How to Successfully Self-Publish & Promote Your Independent Book

A Self-Publishing & Business Marketing Guide
For The Independent Author

by Aaron Ryan
Bestselling author of the *"Dissonance"* sci-fi alien invasion quadrilogy, the work-life balance business book *"The Superhero Anomaly,"* and the sci-fi thriller *"Forecast"*

For Sweeps, Bren & AJ:
Thank you for putting up with me.
And for editing me.

© 2024 Aaron Ryan & CM LLC. U.S. Copyright # TX 9-405-281. All Rights Reserved. Unauthorized duplication or copying prohibited by law. The scanning, uploading, and distribution of this book via the Internet or via any other means without the express written permission of the publisher or copyright holder is illegal and punishable by law. Please purchase only authorized print or electronic versions and do not participate in or encourage electronic piracy of copyrighted materials.

Published in 2024, Edition 1.

ISBN # 9798990878952.

Cover art by Trivuj.

Edited by CM LLC. Published independently.

PREFACE

Strap in, because this is going to be a fun and informative ride.

This book is about the incredibly awesome and respectable career choice called *writing* or *authoring*, how you can start a career providing it, and ultimately, become tremendously successful at it.

It's not about book writing itself, the technique of it, preferred software to write in, crafting particular styles of narratives, particular genres, your own personal idiosyncrasies of how you write, etc.. It's about the business of *writing,* and running a sound business

Being an author has rocked my world and changed my life…forever. I mean that.

Who am I? I am Aaron Ryan (said in my best "I'm Batman" voice.) Without going too much in-depth here, I'll refer you to the "About the Author" section. Suffice it to say that I want this book to be about how you get properly started and successful as a self-published author, as opposed to being about me.

However, briefly…

I am a middle-aged guy who's been doing authoring off and on since the second grade, way back in 1981, which should tell you how very old I am, so please erase that from your memory. I've been an author and voiceover artist since 1993. I made the jump to self-employment in 2007. Up until that point I had been (and still am) a successful multimedia businessman who ran five different companies from the comfort of his home. Now, it sometimes takes money to make money, and so my situation is a bit unique, as I had money going into authoring. Before I ever launched out into doing them full time, I had already generated over a million dollars in revenue from my multimedia production company. Therefore, my situation is not tremendously representative of the overwhelming majority of those seeking to enter into authoring *or* voice acting. In many ways, I am an anomaly. Because of this, I promise to approach everything I describe from as much of a layman perspective as possible.

I've been very successful in authoring and voice acting, and that success is what motivates me to write. It is what *enables* me to do so. I write prolifically, and this book is essentially my seventeenth book, and my eighth on running effective business and marketing. My writings can be found all over the interwebs under my author name as well as my former voiceover stage name, Josh Alexander: in LinkedIn articles, on Medium.com, on Tumblr, on Facebook, and wherever else they're floating around the ether.

However, authoring is my heart's desire (that and Bottle Caps candy) and, as such, it was my heart's desire to write more about it. I *love* writing: and for a time it was my goal to be the Dave Barry of voiceover bloggers and authors, offering good quality satire and lightening the load through edutainment. Now I just write to inspire, equip, and take my readers on a journey through my fiction books.

The author of this book has been a telemarketer, a Dairy Queen clerk, an office manager, an administrative assistant, an audio editor, a dispatcher, a Christian singer & speaker, a Jack in the Box worker, a paperboy, a corporate and wedding videographer, a service manager, a paperboy *again*, an author, an artist, a poet, a business owner, a blogger, a graphic and web designer, and a dancer. I dropped dancing many years and many pounds ago when it became painfully obvious that I was about as graceful as a drunken lumbering Brachiosaurus traversing a field of marbles. I humbly acknowledge that God has given me some indisputable gifts. (Dancing is not one of them. Using mental telepathy on stoplights is.) I am deeply grateful and operate out of a profound sense of gratitude every day because of my gifts. You'll hear that as a constant and driven refrain throughout my book. I've had a lot of experience in a lot of areas since entering the workforce in 1988. I've worked at probably thirty different jobs. None of them will remember me, because I was the guy who wanted to be somewhere else. Who was *bound* to be somewhere else. Who actually *was* somewhere else sometimes, and that's why I was politely asked never to return.

So, back to this book…

Is this book about approaching traditional publishers and agents? No, although I'll touch on that. It's not about that. Is it about writing technique? No. It's about being a successful book publisher, and a successful author *business.* The title of the book is why you purchased this book, or had it forced upon you by your wife who wants you to stop playing around and put some bread on the table. Traditional publishing is for those who want to go that route, who want to be represented. But for the overwhelming rest of all of us, we seek to carve out our own niche, to make our own mark, to stake our own claim, and to put our name out there and market ourselves. Or, we've already approached the trad pub's, and been denied more times than we can count. Either way, this book is for those who look at "self-publishing" and "marketing" and say "blecchhh" – may this book be the Tums to your upset tummy. May it help you defray the specter of both, and understand that it really is much easier than you think.

For the record, we'll be referring a lot to KDP, or Kindle Direct Publishing, through this book a lot, as well as Ingram Spark, and Draft2Digital, as examples. Additionally, as my experience is mostly with the USA market, the overwhelming majority of the content in here is focused in that direction. However, many elements should translate internationally just fine.

This is a book on taking that craft and putting it on a moving vehicle to take it somewhere: the vehicle of a successful business. More on mentoring later, but here's what you'll learn from a great mentor:

- Industry insights
- Places to promote
- Recommended hardware and software
- Writing technique
- Design and layout of your books
- More

Please ensure that you don't skip mentoring – it's so critical to your success as an author!

Well, then, is this book about business development and self-publishing only? No. I certainly didn't want to be solely an informational writer: there are plenty of those out there already, and I'd just be joining the choir. Nay. I wanted to also bring some humor and some levity to your journey that is sometimes fraught with "rejection" (which is actually just selection: they didn't 'reject' you; they just 'selected' someone else's book) so that you can recharge at this pit-stop called laughter, and find strength to go another mile and send those auditions. So, know that you're embarking on an eclectic read that won't be just scholarly lecture-like. I deeply love Dave Barry, Steven Wright, Demetri Martin and Mitch Hedberg humor, and so some of my material is written in somewhat of a lighthearted and comical style to balance out the information overload that you may experience in other chapters.

Conversely, it really, *really* impresses me when I develop a relationship with someone that is based on frequent exchanges of humor, when we finally sit down and have a cup of coffee together and there it is: that immense cavernous well of depth that they possessed, which I had to date received only hints of. People are *so* interesting, and there is so much more than meets the eye. I hate having one without the other. Purely shallow comedic exchanges leave you craving more connection and depth; too much emphasis on the heavy depth leaves you wanting to come up for air. So, this book offers both some comedic interludes *and* business insight to give you that well-rounded view.

> **Business is a serious thing, and while you can get by on levity, you can't advance without sincerity.**

I regard my situation humbly. When I'm following in the greats like JRR Tolkien, CS Lewis, Suzanne Collins, Isaac Asimov, Marie Lu, James S.A. Corey, and so many more, I don't know what I can truthfully add to the babble (because that's what we do all day) of voices that hasn't already been mentioned somewhere along the line. But I'm sure going to try. After all, I'm a try-er. Especially of patience. Ask my wife. I have never really played by the rules. I don't like rules. See? That's me driving over there on the other side of the highway with the crap-eating grin on my face. Wave! Wave to the nice men with the handcuffs driving right behind me! Such nice men with handcuffs.

I tend to buck the establishment and try the *Kobiyashi Maru*[1] approach. I'm unconventional that way, and thus, may seem controversial at times. I'm ok with it. My motto in business has always been "adapt and overcome."

Case in point: in 2007 I was besieged by a Craigslist flagger who decided to for whatever reason single out my media production ads and flag them repeatedly for removal. This was prior to Craigslist revamping their flagging policies. This continued from January through March of 2007. After three months of frustration, it prompted me to create a brand-new *alternative* website for the very same services I was providing… and thus I created different ads…and thus the flagger didn't even know those ads were mine…and thus he left me alone…and thus I said "thus" a lot.

Adapt and overcome.

The sad truth is that his email address (we engaged in delightfully angry dialogue after he intentionally reached out to lecture me about my postings) was *flagger.cl@gmail.com*. Talk about a pathetic identity: it was his *calling* to ruin others. The same is true of people on Reddit who, once you've posted a positive offer to help those seeking to learn about authoring, downvote your answer. Why on earth you would downvote a post seeking to help people is beyond me. Some people in this world simply perplex me, whether they're serial flaggers or downvoters.

It is an unfortunate reality that sad, skeptical cynics are so pervasive on social media that they'll do anything to subvert a good cause out of their own suspicious worldview. I guess it takes a wide variety of people to populate a planet. Oh well! I'll be over here adapting and overcoming while they're over there hating people.

You now hold this book in your hands because you're either:

- A. exploring writing for the first time, or
- B. exploring *improving* your writing career, and you're ready to publish, or preparing to publish, a book you've written

Either way, I applaud you. To quote that great prophet Obi-Wan Kenobi, "You've just taken your first step into a larger world."

This book is a diary of lessons learned. It's a collection of business tips and tricks. It's a compendium of everything I've learned in business to make me successful as an author, and everything I employ today to make -and keep- me successful. And I've indeed been successful! At the time of this writing:

- I've generated over $3.3 million dollars in overall business since 2003
- In my highest revenue month ever, I brought in $67,250 in combined income from my authoring and voiceovers.
- As of mid-June 2004, I've sold nearly two-thousand of my books online and offline. That's an average of three-hundred sixty three books per month!

All of this gets me very, very excited. It's insane! Sometimes I wake up laughing. I'm very excited about my future forecast, and being able to eat lobster for dinner every night, on authoring money. In fact, the only thing that remains is to record authoring *while* eating lobster, at which point I will surely die from ecstasy.

I am *passionate* about life, and I am *passionate* about writing. In essence, it has nothing short of rescued me from being trapped in a career I loathed. I was performing wedding videography, which is the same as floating in a pot of boiling acid and being forced to listen to Michael Bolton on a punishing loop. Authoring has also saved me from the 9-to-5 doldrums and ratcheted up my confidence and drive to succeed. I live, sleep, eat, drink, and breathe writing.

Nothing has ever motivated me like writing has, and it's to the point where I loathe Friday afternoons (because the workweek is ending) and I am leg-shakingly excited on Sunday evenings (because the workweek is about to start). Wow. In fact, if you hover over me when I'm sleeping, and say the word "author," I'm sure to wake up with a jubilant thrill! Several people have been arrested for trying: it's been entertaining! Such nice men with handcuffs.

What I love about self-employment is that it's *mine*. No one can take it from me. I rise and fall on my own merits, and whether or not I succeed is completely up to me, not my employer's paycheck. I am pursuing *my* dreams, not my employer's. That, to me, is something I will never willingly trade, and you'd have to pry from my cold, dead, typewriter-gripping hands.

It's my hope that the book I'm writing is filled to the brim with new and exciting material, and of course great humor. But in truth, I can only draw upon those who have gone before me, and couple that with the very best of what I know. So, do me a favor and pretend to be excited if you hear something that's been heard before, and I'll promise to Thesaurus-it-up to give it a fresh spin for you, and try to perhaps make it a little more memorable. Business is a serious thing, and while you can get by on levity, you can't genuinely advance without intentionality.

It is with great deference and respect that I undertake to write about the business of writing and of successfully publishing your book, and share it with you, because I'm treading on sacred ground of learning, and in that sacred process, *yea verily*, the student becometh the teacher.

Am I qualified to speak on writing, and running a writing business? My numbers don't lie: the truth is yes. I've been interviewed countless times. I am constantly thanked by budding and established writing talent the world over for their inspiration in social circles. My books have sold well. I've put out a lot of books that people buy. I will go forth humbly and with honor, and with great cognizance that the ones who went before me equipped me to write the very book I'm writing, and I draw from them in the sharing.

The last thing I would say, in a bit of a disclaimer, is that this book is written from *my* perspective. It is what has worked for *me*; it may not necessarily work for you. In fact, it's guaranteed to *not* work for some people, because no one is quite like me (that's my wife saying 'thank God' in the background), and no one has the same makeup that I do. I operate how I operate and have perfected my approach to code of conduct that works in tandem with my own makeup, which is a lovely shade of rouge, with thick mascara, enabling me to bat my eyes at you and make you, in the words of Antonio Banderas, ess-swoon.

That being said, what I've provided in this book comes from *years* of successful self-publishing, and *years* of successful marketing and business operations, and I'm glad to share all of this with you through the lens of application toward a writing career.

Authoring is an industry that has drastically changed and been upended. Some say in a bad way, some say in a good way. And even more say in a *weird* way. With the advent of the Internet, AI, ChatGPT and more, everyone can be an author. You can publishing a book in a *day.* The bar to entry is very, very low, and it is a very easy industry to enter...and a very difficult industry to get right...unless you have direction and are highly committed to your dream.

My friend, the wonderful voice talent and author Paul Strikwerda, highlights the difference between those interested and those committed:

*"The interested person is merely exploring options. The committed person is going for it. The interested person says: 'I'd like to,' 'I'm thinking of' 'It would be nice…"
The committed person says, 'This is my path,' 'This is my passion,' 'Nothing can stop me.' The interested person reactively responds to opportunities. The committed person proactively creates opportunities. The interested person is not invested in the outcome. The committed person does whatever it takes to achieve the outcome. The interested person is conditioned to 'trying.' The committed person is conditioned to 'doing.' The interested person always has reasons. The committed person has results."*[2]

Everyone wants to hop on board The Love Train.

A sea change has come to the authoring industry, revolutionizing and equipping thousands to pursue their dream of writing. What does that mean for you? Four words:

YOU. CAN. DO. THIS.

You are a vertebrate, not an invertebrate. *pause for effect* Wait what? Yes, you heard me. You have spine. You have backbone. You have fortitude comprising your very frame.. You're not a slippery fish or a spineless coward. You have decided to pursue something *rife* with rejection, *fraught* with fear, and *simmering* in struggle. The struggle as an author is real, but you can do this. I believe in you.

This book is about my own experiences, my own life, my own passion, my own insights, and my own joy, as seen through a business and career as an author. And I want to share it with you! *Tres bien, no?* Will everything herein apply to you? Certainly not. Will it be a fun trek though? Most definitely.

I've *so* enjoyed writing it, and my fingers hurt from so much typing, but it's a good hurt. I hope you enjoy it too, because I couldn't wait to share it with all of you…for a small fee of course. (My wife feels that our children need to eat.)

And now I'll say to you what Glenne Headley's character *The Jackal* said in *Dirty Rotten Scoundrels*: *"Ready? Then let's go get 'em."*

CONTENTS

PREFACE 7
CONTENTS 21
CHAPTER 1: AND THEY'RE OFF! 23
CHAPTER 2: WRITING: A HORRIBLE HOBBY 43
CHAPTER 3: CREATING & SUSTAINING A THRIVING WRITING BUSINESS 53
CHAPTER 4: MARKETING & VISIBILITY FOR YOUR WRITING BUSINESS 93
CHAPTER 5: SUCCESSFULLY PROMOTING YOUR SELF-PUBLISHED BOOK 125
CHAPTER 6: NETWORKING & MENTORING 147
CHAPTER 7: TO AI OR NOT TO AI: THAT IS THE QUESTION 165
CHAPTER 8: THE PROCESS OF SELF-PUBLISHING ... 171
CONCLUSION 185
ABOUT THE AUTHOR 191
MORE BOOKS BY AARON RYAN 193
RECOMMENDED READING 197
BIBLIOGRAPHY 199

CHAPTER 1: AND THEY'RE OFF!

Before you jump right into it and scream to the world from the rooftops, *"I'M GOING TO BE THE GALAXY'S GREATEST AUTHOR AND THAT'S THAT! HEAR ME ROAR, WORLD!!!"* have you sat down and asked yourself if you really do have what it takes?

If not, are you willing to train, to learn, and to study, to get it?

Jeff Goldblum's character in Jurassic Park had a line that I will never forget. It goes as follows: "Yeah, yeah, but your scientists were so preoccupied with whether or not that they *could*, that they didn't stop to think if they *should.*" So I want to ask you from the very beginning to ask yourself, *should* you do this? *Should* you publish that book? You might very well be able to, but *should* you? Will it become a passing fancy? Or might you spend so much money in it and ultimately be unsuccessful, angry, and in debt? All things to consider before launching out into this field and publishing / promoting your book. This is not to dissuade you! If you believe in your book, then by all means, plunge headlong forth to success.

With that said, let me congratulate you on even *considering* taking such an awesome plunge. You're about to dive into a pool full of wonder, great accomplishment, hopes fulfilled, character-driven flamboyancy, awesome networking, incredible dreams realized, and endless possibilities of being chosen.

There are plenty of genres you can pursue as an author. You can pursue:

- Fiction
- Non-Fiction
- And, well, pretty much anything else that is neither fiction nor non-fiction.

See? Plenty.

Authoring is a behemoth of an industry, continually poised for growth despite the threats to it such as AI and the continuing erosion of selling power. Regarding AI, even as OpenAI, ChatGPT and other assistive apps have grown in popularity, the truth is that people still prefer the emotional connection of a real human artist[3]. Once they find out that a computer authored your book, and you're merely profiting off of that? Ick.

"How do I get started as an author?" is a question that has been asked by millions of people. Just search Quora[4] and you'll see what I mean. "How do I self-publish?" pops up all the time. Home writing studios crop up all the time and authors dot the planet numbering in the hundreds of thousands. And that question has been answered by many of these people with "I did it, and it worked."

Maybe you're asking this question because you've been told "you have talent as an author." Many people have expressed to me that people have told them that. I want to start by saying something that might surprise you. Here it is: *"So what?"* And yes, I meant to say that. Is it a mean question? Not really, when you think about it. Every field needs to validate its entrants, and the authoring industry is no exception.

- Resilience
- A lot of skill
- The ability to network
- A sense of humor
- The willingness to fail...and then try again
- The willingness to face rejection
- Allowing yourself to be mentored and trained
- Business acumen
- Listening
- Imparting
- Being passionate
- Putting power behind your words
- Determination
- Grit
- Foresight
- Planning
- Marketing
- and most of all, being committed to goals.

BOOK DESIGN

The first thing we need to talk about is book design. Do you already have that worked out? Do you have graphic design skills? If not, **get a book designer.** You'll thank me later. People still judge a book by its cover, and they will yours, bet your bottom dollar. Your book can have the greatest content inside; but people won't read it unless the cover so draws them to itself irresistibly. If you're able to design your own cover, great. More power to you. But by all means run that cover past a multitude of people, as well as professional publishers and agents, and see what they say. Your mom may like it; will the reader? Your mom will buy one copy and tell her fifty friends. Readers might buy it by the millions, and they'll tell their million friends.

GOALS & GROWTH

Here's what I say, and many would agree. The very first thing that you need to do is contact a writing mentor. Don't wait. Join a Facebook group, post something about needing a mentor, and see who will be willing to answer your questions and take you under their wing. You don't know everything there is to know yet! Neither did I. Neither *do* . A mentor will give it to you straight, and they'll tell you how it is.

Remember this formula well:

Mentoring > Knowledge > Application > Promotion

Get mentoring. *Get instruction on how to do this right.* Everything else hinges on that. Do NOT skip mentoring. You'll then have the knowledge to do it right. Then you'll be able to put that knowledge into practice. And then? You're ready to start promoting the product that you sought mentoring about how to promote in the first place. Follow this foundation, and you'll succeed.

Aside from that, network with other authors. Join groups online. There are Facebook groups aplenty, full of so many, many more, who would be willing to sow into your lives. I'm part of the "Authors & Writers ONLY" group on Facebook, and I help admin it. It's a wonderful group. Others, like "The Writers Forum" and "Authors Supporting Authors" are fantastic communities to join.

Join local authoring Meetups. Talk with others in online communities. Network, network, network. Rub shoulders with greatness, and greatness will rub off on you.

DON'T QUIT YOUR DAY JOB

Ever heard that phrase? Lots of people the world over have been told "don't quit your day job." It's a phrase that is not meant to deter, and is often said in a spirit of humor. Ultimately, lots of actors (voice and regular actors alike) have to find a way to pay the bills. And voice acting won't do that right out of the gate. Ever heard the label "Starving Artist"? Mm-hmm.

There are celebrities in the authoring world who make a *fortune* and an absolute *killing* as an author. There are legends. Names like Tolkien. Collins. Rowling. Asimov. Foster. S.A. Corey. Ryan. (kidding on that last one! 😊) Or master authors who may have held you captive, spellbound, as they have shared their story with you.

All of these people have invested into their craft, and spent countless time and dollars perfecting what they do and how they do it. Their names are fairly synonymous with celebrity, because they've paved the way.

But they didn't just make a killing as an author right away. They worked very hard to pay for the things that they needed, such as equipment, mentoring, software, training, and marketing. So, after a mentor, remember that you need to make sure to find a way to pay for the things that you're going to need to be successful as an author. To do that, you're going to need to make or save some cash, and invest that right back into your career. You'll need money for:

> *Do NOT skip mentoring. You'll then have the knowledge to do it right. Then you'll be able to put that knowledge into practice. And then? You're ready to start promoting the product that you sought mentoring about how to promote in the first place. Follow this foundation, and you'll succeed.*

- A good working computer(s)

- Cloud services if you want your documents in the cloud
- Membership to things like QueryTracker for submitting to agents and publishers
- Advertising budget
- Promotions services
- Advertising budget for ads on social media
- Book Cover Designers
- Other Graphic designers
- Editors & Proofreaders
- Advertisement optimizers
- Advertising materials for trade shows, if you want to do that (banners, displays, canopy, table, etc.) – these make a standard booth shine!
- Author copies of your books
- Membership to online payment processors to accept ecommerce
- And more

I've heard it said that a career in cosmetology costs you between fifteen and twenty-five thousand dollars. And what do you get paid for a haircut? $18? $40? $60? You can author a book that will go viral, and then millions of people will buy it if it does that. For a minimal investment!

Which one will you choose? Take your time; I'll be here when you come to your senses. A career as an author could be incredibly lucrative…and residual! If you author a book once and then it takes off and sells itself? That's residual income, baby.

ARE YOU A SELF-PROMOTER?

There's nothing wrong with a little shameless self-promotion here and there. In this industry, the readers aren't going to necessarily find you. You have to work to find *them*. You have to *humbly put aside your humble*. Stick your chest out. Inhale deeply and know that you're a force to be reckoned with. After all, will the sheepish "Uh, sorry to bother you, but I was wondering if *[insert desperate plea here]*" approach get you anywhere? Methinks not.

Know deep inside, or at least start down the *path* of knowing and accepting, that you are a contender. That you are talented, and have something to offer. Be a unique voice. Oscar Wilde said, "Be yourself; everyone else is already taken." Find your unique voice and tell your own unique story. There is nothing outside of the realm of possibility when you take on this mantle and don this cape. You are a *Writing Superhero.* Believe it right now.

Take the time to figure out where and how you're going to market, and know that there are people who will help you. I'm one of them. Be bold. Know that you're in the ring and you have something to offer.

BUT AARON, WHERE CAN I MARKET?

You can market your book *everywhere:*

- Trade shows / craft fairs / vendor markets

- LinkedIn
- Alignable
- Instagram
- Facebook
- TikTok
- Quora
- Reddit
- Google Ads
- Amazon Ads
- Instagram ads
- Facebook ads
- TikTok Ads
- Craigslist
- Vimeo
- YouTube
- Tumblr
- Twitter
- Hand out bookmarks to people for free
- Direct Emails
- Blog posts
- Local networking groups such as Meetup, BizBuilders, LeTip, BNI, and Chambers of Commerce.
- Local bookstores AND national chains with a local branch who are amenable to hosting local authors for a book signing
- Talk to other authors about where and how they market
- SO many more places

Everywhere you look, possible book buyers are swarming around you, under your nose, rubbing shoulders with you, sitting next to you, driving in front of you (or tailgating you), on the bus with you, on the phone with you, *in your life with you*. Authoring can be plugged into every area of your life. One of the best ways you can reach out is by getting vinyl lettering on your car...or having branded T-Shirts made that instruct people to "ask me about writing." Seriously! Think I'm crazy? I've done both, and I've driven that car and worn that T-shirt out *on date night*. You never know who you might run into - and even if it's not a potential book buyer, what better subject to talk about than your exciting career?? (Or perhaps your amazing children, time permitting...)

Be an *enthusiast*. No one will sell you better than you. And no one will know what you do unless what you're wearing, what you're driving - unless *you* - tell them what you do.

Seriously, they're all out there. And my wife even lets me wear that shirt on date night without getting angry.

BUT WHAT ABOUT BUSINESS SAVVY?

Now. That little thing called "business acumen". This is where a lot of authors fall short and drop off the map. Business savvy. Acumen. Do you know what it means?

What does it take for you to run a successful writing business? Surely, you can't run it with just your typing fingers. You need a system in place *around* your fingers to ensure that that beautiful little product you're trying so hard to peddle is getting heard, getting estimated properly, getting invoiced properly, and reaching people. You need to have a structure around this enterprise called "my writing."

I've designed stationery. This includes:

- Business cards
- Logo
- Glossies
- T-Shirts
- Vinyl stickers on my car windows
- Thank you cards
- Bookmarks
- Flyers

I've needed to treat my writing business *like a business*. If I treat it like a hobby, it might make a bit of bucks for a coffee here and there. However, if I treat it like a business, I can make some exceptionally good revenue. There's a huge chasm of difference between some extra chump change, and genuine hard-earned, measurable revenue. One is a side hustle; the other is a thriving enterprise.

You need to think about what your *business* is going to look like for self-publishing your book. Can you envision yourself as, instead of a writer, a successful businessperson who just *happens* to write? If you can do the latter, you're going places. Remember: *failing to plan is planning to fail.*

WHAT'S YOUR NEXT MOVE?

Get some great books to help you learn! These are some *super* books available out there:

- *Making Money in Your PJs* by Paul Strikwerda[5]
- *The Superhero Anomaly by Yours Truly*
- *How to Self-Publish a Children's Book* by Yvonne Jones[6]
- *How to Publish a Book on Amazon in 2024*[7]
- Successful Self-Publishing by Joanna Penn[8]
- MANY others

And remember what I said? Contact a mentor. That's your very first step. When I first launched into writing, I was so shocked to find such a community of such sustained support, and an environment of help out there. That community and environment has grown substantially with the internet. It has ballooned.

Authors genuinely want other authors to succeed! It's such a strange industry that way - where you encourage your competitor to get a job that you're in the running for. Plumbers don't do that. Automotive shops don't do that. Electricians don't do that.   Realtors don't do that.

Just know that you can do this. The caveat is that you both have an equal footing. Just because Joe Author has 26 years' experience, and you have 26 minutes', doesn't automatically grant Joe Author *fait accompli*. The reader just may have *your* voice in their heads...not Mr. Author's, regardless of your lack of experience. If you write like you've breathed life into your words, and you can powerfully sculpt something people want to read, then you just might outsell an industry pro.

This is an industry that is tremendous fun. There are incredible annual events and conferences[9]. You can join regular local authoring Meetups and be inspired by your fellow colleagues and this mutual race of shared joy and pursuit. Cheer on and be cheered! Encourage and be encouraged! Authoring are a rewarding career on a number of levels, even before you score your first job.

Why?

The benefits of being an author:

- Work from home
- Work as much or as little as you like
- Set your own hours
- Spend time with your family and your own pursuits
- Have a career that you can call your own
- Be creative
- Call your own shots
- Choose your own readers
- Constantly grow and innovate in performing and marketing
- Take longer-than-two-week vacations
- And, the most awesome....write in your underwear. (Ew.)

Sound appealing? It should. It's the best life ever.

I hope this answers the question "How do I get started as an author?" for you. Ultimately, just start. It's fun in this sandbox.

All this goes without saying that this is from *my* experience. Everyone's experiences are unique to *them*. However, if you would like a much more robust experience than this one - and a much longer, comprehensive resource guide - check out an article I've enjoyed on Indeed[10].

GIVING IT YOUR ALL

I recently had a conversation with a colleague, and they were telling me that they don't ever really give their "all" during their drafts; they save it for the actual final writing. I had to scoff at their logic, for obvious reasons. I literally made a scoff sound, which sounds something like a cross between a gag and a profound urge to pee. Huh? Saving it for the actual writing? *Mon ami*, you'll never get to the actual writing without giving it your *all* to get there….without a powerful foundation.

You can't get a 100% book from a 50% draft.

THE READER'S CHAIR

Let's look at it from the reader's perspective for a moment. You know they're developing book fatigue as they go through the onslaught of submitted books. You know they're losing the will to live as they *next-next-next* their way through scores of them. Is it reasonable to assume that you, appearing in their lineup with your half-baked and noncommittal draft, are going to make the slightest impression on their reading choice?

You might have heard of the "log line" or the "book blurb." Michael Bell, a voice actor, says the following:

One thing I've learned is that your VO audition must capture the casting director's attention in the first 10 seconds or they will not listen to the rest. They simply don't have time.[11]

The same is true for authors in regard to their book! You never get a second chance to make a first impression, right? One of the best log lines I ever came up with for my books was for *Dissonance Volume Zero: Revelation*, my prequel to my alien invasion sci-fi trilogy:

> *We thought they were angelic messengers.*
> *We were wrong.*

Send a chill down your spine? Your log line should do the same. It's the hook, the magnet, and the tractor beam. Michael Bell is right. If you don't capture their attention, you're a goner. You're literally *dead in the water*, and the reader will never even remember your name. You'll never even get to the good stuff before your book is shot down.

But how about this. How about if you, with all of your muster and luster and bluster, can take that draft, supercharge it, and make such an impression you're your final version will be full of weight and incredibly powerful?

Your goal is to knock 'em dead. Not to knock 'em somewhat sleepy.

ALL OR NUTTIN'

Armageddon. Lord of the Rings. Mission Impossible. Raiders of the Lost Ark. The Empire Strikes Back. Cujo. Close Encounters of the Third Kind. Taken. Tootsie. Aliens. Meet the Parents. E.T.. Finding Nemo. Star Wars. Blair Witch Project. It's a Wonderful Life. The Goonies.

Name *any* movie, and you will recognize that there's a plot. A goal. An important mission. The protagonist(s) in any movie has a task that they must accomplish, and they must go on a journey of self-discovery in order to get there. They have to go on a journey of change; they have to grow and learn. They're committed to their goal and their mission.

> ***Your goal is to knock 'em dead. Not to knock 'em somewhat sleepy.***

Just because you're not at screenplay stage yet, should your draft be with any less feeling?

Remember *The Return of the* King, the movie? I will never forget one of the last scenes. Sam and Frodo are halfway up Mount Doom. Sam says to a fading Frodo, "C'mon, Mr. Frodo. I can't carry it for you. But I can carry you! *Come on!*" And Sam slings Frodo over his shoulder and carries him all the way up Mount Doom. Half-baked food doesn't taste very good. Half-assed attempts don't resonate with anyone.

If your goal is to get in, why would you be content with just quietly knocking at the front door?

There's so much more to say on this – but is there? Is it really necessary? It's simple. There's no getting around it. You can't *almost* your way into a successful book. You can't *kind of* do it. You *intend* your way into a role. Otherwise, you intend your way into frustration.

I HAVE A LOT TO GIVE. SO, HERE'S A LITTLE BIT

Every draft, every time, in every way, requires everything you've got. So, live up to your investment and promise.

Chew on these examples:

- Baseball's heavy hitters don't swing for the infield, hoping to lazy-lob one.
- Wide receivers don't race across the field, planning to run underneath the ball without raising their arms to catch it.

- Basketball players don't charge down the court, wanting to just stand under the hoop.
- Politicians don't run for the presidency just so they can increase their Twitter followers.
- Top chefs don't strive to make the best Top Ramen.
- Tourists don't go to Rome and hope to avoid the Coliseum.
- Fishermen don't cast their line out, wishing for minnows.
- The Beatles didn't take their music to America, desiring to play only in garages and talent shows.

Authors don't hope to do a mildly acceptable job. Is it risky to give your all and put yourself out there?
Sure. But the cold truth? You have more to risk by *not* risking. It's called giving your *all*. It's called going the distance. They call it 100%.

There's no such thing as conserving your energy in draft writing. The draft maketh the smash hit. Go forth therefore, and give thou in all thy fullness! *disengages King James mode*

STREAMLINE YOUR PROCESS

Streamline your draft! Don't spend precious minutes, hours, whatever, endlessly writing and rewriting and then editing and re-editing. Write powerfully, yes! But write smartly, and don't second-guess yourself as you go along. I love what Jordan Peele said, "When I'm writing the first draft I'm constantly reminding myself that I'm simply shoveling sand in to a box so that later I can build castles." Shovel that sand intentionally, and prepare to write your own castles.

Don't get stuck in analysis paralysis. Don't spin your wheels on your writing and second-guess yourself. If you suffer from imposter syndrome, surround yourself with people who will counter that for you and edify you, showing you where you can improve, and refining you. Trust yourself, do well, develop a template and stick to it. Streamline your workflow, streamline your writing process, get them done, and get them out.

Go forth boldly to your castle, good knight!

CHAPTER 2: WRITING: A HORRIBLE HOBBY

THE *HOBBY* OF WRITING

When you think of a hobby, what comes to mind?

- Playing the drums?
- Sculpting clay?
- Writing poetry?
- Calligraphy?
- Painting?
- Building suspension bridges in your backyard?[12]
- Collecting baseball cards?

What is a hobby, after all, but a pastime? Just that: something to pass the time. It holds no significant long-term value other than personal fulfillment – which I'm not knocking by the way; we need that! – but a hobby brings nothing to your budget; rather it brings *expense* for materials, or training, or other supplies needed to enjoy said hobby. Nothing is added to your career forecast other than a carved-out piece of your schedule dedicated to enjoyment.

> ***Expenses take care of a short-term need; investments produce returns and dividends.***

Authoring, as a hobby, can bring a lot of fulfillment.

It can also *deprive* you of fulfillment. You can settle on the nickel and miss the dollar. It can bring you some measure of satisfaction, and rob you of utter contentment. It can pass the time, and in the same stretch, steal your time, never to return it in the long run.

So, enjoy your authoring hobby! I pray you have fun with it! I hope that it's fulfilling for three weeks, or six months, or perhaps two years. I expect that you'll thoroughly enjoy it and that it fulfills you.

And I pray that you drop it as a *hobby* like a hot potato.

THE *BUSINESS* OF WRITING

If you choose to pursue writing as a hobby, God bless you. No one could blame you: after all, it certainly is an enjoyable one! Hey, you might even make $20 from a book!

Or…you could make $5000. $5,000,000. Residual money forever. Plus name recognition. Plus connections to future book buyers and other writing jobs in abundance. Plus plus plus.

A hobby brings you temporary fulfillment; a business brings you increasing provision. You must treat this like a business if you are to succeed.

Hobbies and crafts are essential for our contentment. Forest Hill Retirement says that they lower the heart rate.[13] They bring us balance and health. They give us the ability to unplug. For me, I sing, I blog, I swim, I run, and I build Lego spaceships with my son. OK, the honest truth is that he's asleep and I've commandeered them to add another sick Lego spaceship to my *kickass* fleet.

But…

What if you could unplug from your 9 to 5, and you could instead make a living off of your "hobby?" What if you could convert it into a business?

If you truly treat expenses (short term) as investments (long term), you'll go far. Everything that you expend with authoring, divesting yourself of finances *today* for something that is an investment into your *tomorrow*, is a decision that catapults you forward into the far future of your progress. You're saying, essentially, "I believe in myself and my abilities to produce this money back, and to in fact grow a money tree that will continue to bear fruit for myself, because of this one [insert purchase here]." Some of your investments are veritable time machines, taking you from here to there in the timeline of quality, leapfrogging intermediate purchases you might have made.

Expenses take care of a short-term need; investments produce returns and dividends.

With authoring as a business, you could gain direct readers & buyers for yourself through enthusiastic promotion and marketing, and secure readers, or an agent, or, eventually, a publisher (if you want that), or a screenwriter, or a movie adaptation, that will bring you multiple thousands of dollars' worth of work per year… half-year…quarter… or even month! On that note, as of this writing, my novel *Dissonance Volume I: Reality*, which is the opener to my trilogy, is being adapted to screen by Alan Roth of Act Two Media[14], and I couldn't be more elated. Can't wait to see how that fleshes out!

On that note, the reason why I self-publish is because I am a self-starter. I don't want to give up creative control, and I don't want it to take forever. Traditional publishers will take your book and publish it, but it might be next year.

> *I never went into authoring with hope…I went in with intention.*

I can do it next day. And traditional publishers likely won't want your materials after they're self-published anyway, because they're already out there. You'd have to pull them and re-approach a publisher. In truth, I approached a publisher who ended up very interested in my work, but here were his words on both traditional publishing AND approaching agents:

> "Honestly, just keep it self-published. I checked out your listing on Amazon, and you're making progress…I don't think you need / want a publisher. No reason to give up the lion's share of your royalties. Most small press, like XXXXXXX (his publishing press), is best suited for people who only want to write. I can take a manuscript from rough draft and pay to get it multiple rounds of professional editing and production, then pay for huge marketing campaigns, all while the author does nothing but write the next book. Then, of course, the publisher

keeps the majority of the royalties. The author benefits by never having to learn the industry (which is a tall task) and never having to lay out $4k+ to produce a professional book…If you can get into traditional publishing like Orbit, Scholastic, or Andrews McMeel, do it. That, however, requires an agent. Getting an agent requires some sort of personal connection. Back in 2016-ish I actually flew across the country for a single 1-hour meeting with a high-power agent. It was my ticket to the big leagues. Without the personal connection, you can't sign an agent. Without an agent, you can't even crack the door into traditional publishing. It is an outdated model that harms both the publisher and the author…In the end, I didn't even sign with the agent I spent $1,000+ to go meet. It wasn't worth it. I was looking at writing an entire new series for the agent to shop, then waiting 1 - 3 years for her to shop the series, then waiting 2 - 4 years for a publisher to produce it. Then, after all that waiting, I'd be looking at 10% royalties. Oh boy. It didn't get me excited. Instead, I wrote the series and self-published it in a year and made twenty grand in 3 months…also, keep in mind that small presses don't have distribution deals for brick and mortar stores. If your goal is the NYT list, you have to sell about 12,000 physical copies at cash registers linked to BookScan (which is about 75% of all bookstore registers). That requires either monstrous success with self-publishing to a degree less than 0.001% ever achieve, or else it requires traditional publishing and a massive marketing campaign. Sadly, even traditionally published authors these days struggle to get their publisher to push the books hard enough to think about the list. That said, the list can be scammed and bought, so does it really matter? I personally put 0 stock in it…Keep doing what you're doing, and then get better at it. Releasing books 2 and 3 will be better marketing than anything else, bar none. So do that first.*

See what I mean? Even a traditional publisher said go the self-publishing route and be great at marketing. Essentially, do what you're doing, and learn from books like this and others. It's unlikely that you'll make the NY Times Bestseller list as an indie writer, but you could – and with elbow grease, hustle, determination and goals, you could make the Amazon bestseller list – and stay there.

Here's what some of my colleagues said about their choice between self and traditional publishing:

"To be honest, I send to traditional publishing and get some really nice rejections. After 6-9 months, I go the self-publishing route. I just want people to read my books. One of my favorites was sending to a place that was looking for 'monsters from the deepest darkest place in your soul.' So, I sent something and the response was, "thank you yada yad, These aren't the monsters we are looking for."

- Author John Hardic

"I tried traditional publishing and after a few hundred rejection letters, said "screw it." I then went to vanity publishing which was a royal pain…and expensive…but I sold enough to pay for itself…which eventually led to a total rewrite of the series and then to self-publishing which lead to 25,000 book sold over a 10 year period. So it's not a fortune in royalties, but enough to pay for the hobby and have fun doing it."

- Author Richard Hurd

"Having a background in film, I wanted to ensure that I retained film rights to my novel so I could have more control when it is made into a movie."

- Author Tirzah Darnell

With self-publishing, I can create everything myself, or have it created, and maintain all creative control. I can negotiate (or just flat out *get*) a higher royalty for each sale. I can choose which formats I make it available in. I can use my own editors and my own designers and my own printers. I choose. I call the shots. That works for me. It may not work for you, in which case you would have to outsource a lot of the prep and creation of the packaging to someone else, but that's okay too. I'm a bit of an all-under-one-roof anomaly in that regard. If you are as well, you should go very far in this industry. Self-starters often do. There's a great article by Publish Drive that highlights the differences as to why you would choose one or the other, at: https://publishdrive.com/self-publishing-vs-traditional-publishing.html

In this vast universe of the internet, with so many players playing the game, all I can focus on is me, and I want to offer quality writing.

TREAT IT LIKE A BUSINESS

Again, I'm a businessman who *happens* to write. I *love* writing books: it is my business, and it is my passion, because the books and the resulting creative works not only bring me joy and fulfillment, they bring me great amounts of resource to provide for my family.

Let me list for you a few things that distinguish me as a businessman, as opposed to a hobbyist:

- I've created two authoring websites to support my business, along with multiple profiles at sites like Amazon, Goodreads, Medium, and more.
- I've invested thousands of dollars into advertising and promotion services because I *believe* in my books.
- I've attended local Meetups and Chambers of Commerce meetings to promote my business
- I obtained business licensing for myself

- I've labeled my car with vinyl lettering to attract business to myself
- I paid for a custom phone number
- I pay taxes on my writing career
- I am constantly seeking to expand my horizons
- Every day, I establish new relationships with potential readers & buyers
- I do this 9 to 5 every weekday, and beyond
- I wake up every day excited to go to work
- I churned out seven books in 2024 alone, and this is one of them.
- When I'm out and about, I make voice memos the instant a new idea comes to me for a blog…a live Instagram video…a workshop…a follow-up note for a buyer…an idea for a book.
- I keep my finger on the pulse of my business with a custom CRM and spreadsheets.
- I am constantly checking my sales metrics
- Every single expense I make into authoring is not that. It is *not* an expense. It is an *investment*.
- I set and hit or exceed goals every week
- I invest time into blogging
- I deliberately give up some weekends throughout the year to do craft fairs and trade shows, lugging around heavy equipment and a huge Pelican case of HEAVY books, because I want people to buy them and enjoy them
- I invest a massive amount of time into marketing
- I've penned a few books on being successful in business across multiple crafts (writing *and* voiceovers)

- I will teach for free at authoring conferences and webinars

I am a writing *businessman* because I choose to make this my business, not my hobby. Again, I never went into authoring with hope…I went in with *intention*. My first step was getting a business license. After that, I could successfully say "It's official!" It was never a hobby, but now it never would be. Yes, I thoroughly enjoy it as one would enjoy a hobby, but I will not relegate authoring to the category of hobby, because there is a huge well there that I can tap in order to bring massive provision to my family.

To relegate authoring to hobby status would be to ricochet off of, to momentarily touch and then leave, and no more, the wonder of a truly satisfying and lucrative career.

BEATING A DEAD HORSE

I'm just another voice in this great choir when I share on this. There are many businessmen just like myself who just happen to write books, but they are first and foremost entrepreneurs. They understand that in order to succeed, you need structure, planning, goal-setting, etc.

You need drive, determination, and resilience. You need focus, clarity of vision, and aptitude. You must find what works best for you as a business, and then run with it. I don't mean to beat a dead horse, so I'll just chime in and say, "What they said." *[pause for effect]*

OK, I'll say even more.

Treat writing like a *business*, make it official, and see yourself reap invaluable rewards heaped upon invaluable rewards.

I'll never forget the first time I was paid for a book I sold. I thought to myself, "Holy smokes, it actually works!" I expected it to, but that feeling opened up Pandora's box within me. Simultaneously, I thought "It's possible." "This is it." "This is where my income will come from."

This system *does* work. It's not Amway, it's not a Ponzi scheme, and it's not a Kool-Aid stand. This is an official business that brings in billions of dollars a year in advertising and other forms of revenue industrywide across multiple genres of books. You can share in those dollars! This system can pay your bills, your car payment, your mortgage, and then some.

It *is* possible.

Go forth and conquer…with a business license.

CHAPTER 3: CREATING & SUSTAINING A THRIVING WRITING BUSINESS

MY STORY

We're going to dive into a lot of informative bits here that hopefully will give you lots of tips and tricks to run a successful writing business long-term.

I'm very humbled to be able to do what I do. I am extraordinarily grateful. It is a tremendous privilege to be able to perform, teach about and blog about writing. They say, "find what you love to do, and you'll never work a day in your life." That's very, very true. I don't "work" at all. 😊 My day does not feel like work. It does not consist of work. Yes, there are activities that I do every day for the maintenance of my writing business. But none of it has ever felt like, "Oh, this is labor". My *wife* has gone through labor. *She* knows what labor is. *This ain't labor.* I absolutely love what I do. And it's a passion of mine. And so, it's my privilege and my joy to share it with you.

Some of my esteemed writing colleagues know that I come from a career in wedding videography. I have essentially been rescued, delivered, so to speak, from a business that negatively impacted my life and sanity. *Hallelujah* for deliverance from bridezillas, groomzillas, momzillas, and all kinds of other -zillas.

Sure, wedding videography fit the bill for a while. It put food on our table. Ultimately it was productive and sustaining, but never emotionally satisfying in the way that writing has been. So, I'm actually not doing that anymore, having given it up in 2018. I am *so* grateful that I've no longer needed it.

How I got into writing was kind of an accident. I was given a writing assignment in the second grade, circa 1981. I wrote a small novella entitled "The Electric Boy." It was complete with drawings that I rendered as well, such as only a second grader can do. The stick figures were perfection. And the story wasn't half bad either! But that set me on a path to writing from a young age. I thank Mrs. Walker for assigning that little task, because it filled me with hopes and dreams. The sad part is that my mom kept that for many years (along with report cards and grade school parapharnelia), and then gave it to me. Wouldn't you know it, I can't find it since we moved! Grrrr.

There's a richness and a trove of opportunities for you to market your book that are just waiting for you. They're ripe for the picking. It is possible with hard work and a little elbow grease, and with grit and gumption, tenacity and resolution.

I average around a thousand to three thousand words typing a day. By mid-2024, I had churned out seven books. And I call that accomplishment. Also, I will never *ever* use AI to write a book for me. I think that's lazy, corner-cutting, and juvenile, frankly. You have the power to create! Why would you surrender that to a machine? It's called *artificial* intelligence for a reason. Artificial isn't real. *You* are real. Never surrender your God-given gift to create. In short, if it AIn't human, then it AIn't for me. #savehumanity #saynotoai #verifiedhuman

It's very possible to write a bestselling book. That's the optimum end result. Here are some screenshots from my "Dissonance" sci-fi quadrilogy, several of which became bestsellers!

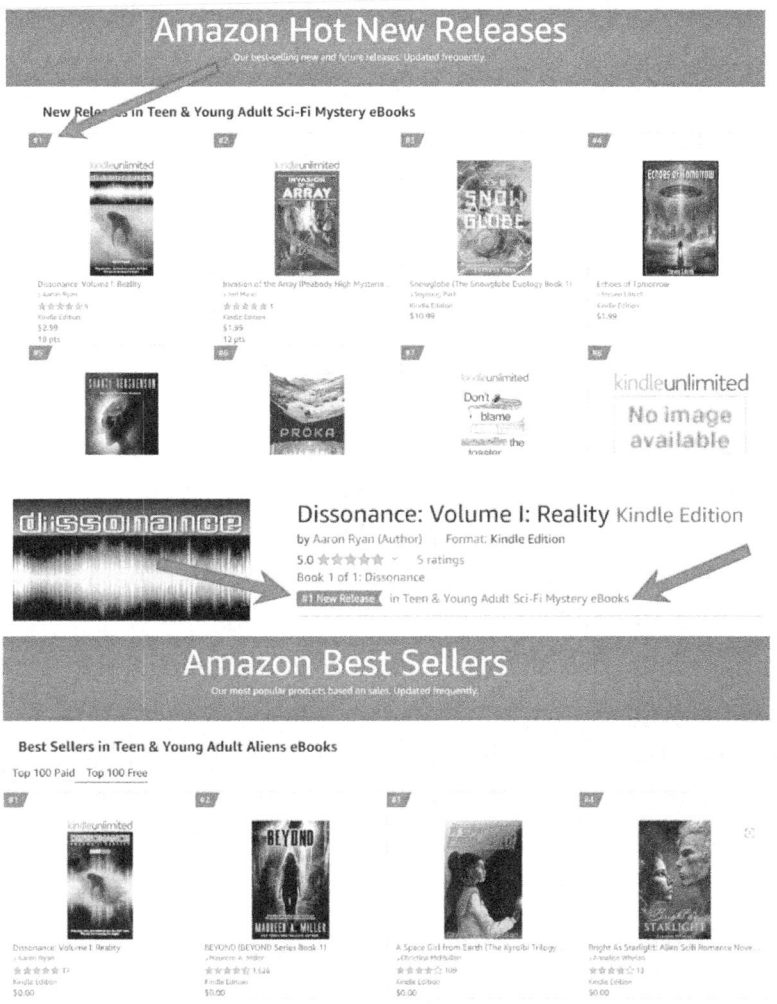

That last one is when I ran a free promotion. People snatched it up! However, I'll never offer anything I write for free again. I just don't believe in it. People *love* to hoard. They love to gather and accumulate. Unfortuntately, that doesn't translate well to them leaving reviews or enjoying your book. They may not even read it. They just simply snatched it up because it was free. That didn't do anything for my standings except temporarily, and it didn't do anything for reviews left for my books. It's up to you if you want to run a free promotion through Kindle Unlimited or otherwise, but for me, it's something that I didn't reap any benefit from, nor do I suspect you will. The higher point, however, is that I value my work too much to give it away for free.

The ultimate goal is to become a bestseller, and to have your books sell like hotcakes. I've achieved number one several times, and I'm so grateful for that. Now, did it last forever? No. Sometimes, only days. And that's perfectly okay. Books rise and fall, up and down the chain. Each sale pushes them up…each space in between pushes them down. Ebbs and flows; so goes life. It's totally fine with me. It is always my dream and goal for a book to go viral, and that should be your dream and goal as well, and work to that end.

So, as you can see, there are five possible beneficial outcomes for me that come from auditions. That's why I do so many per week. I want to get cast for these jobs. That's the ultimate goal. It is *so* rewarding to see that happen.

I currently admin the "Authors & Writers ONLY" group on Facebook; you can join us at https://www.facebook.com/groups/authorsandwriters. It's a thriving community with strong growth and great interaction between members. I also run a group local to Seattle so that we can get together in person, so if you're in Seattle or the Pacific Northwest, you can visit https://www.facebook.com/groups/pugetsoundseattleauthorsandwriters – that's a great one too, although much smaller.

For either group, you can go there and ask questions on equipment, tactics, writing help, ideas, support and affirmation, resources, recommended promotions, self-publishing approaches, conferences, mentoring, plugins, books, resources, technique, whatever. It's a great hive-mind of people prepared to contribute to your success, answer questions honestly, give you feedback on your books and covers, refer you to an excellent mentor, etc. These groups are wonderful. They're strong, thriving, growing communities that can help you.

I've never once – to my recollection – been told, "hey, Aaron, you write good stuff. You should become a writer." I don't recall ever once having been told that. What I'd like for you to focus on in this book is being a *businessperson* first.

Again, I am a businessman who just *happens* to write. In structure, ecosystem, branding, marketing, etc., you can be a contender in the author marketplace, by treating it like a business.

In my voiceover career, I don't like to narrate a lot of audiobooks (except my own books of course!), but I have a reader named Thibaut Meurisse. He is French. He's a wonderful author, in the vein of Anthony Robbins: personal motivation, speaker and author…he once said *"success is not an event, success is a process"*.

What a fantastic quote! Success is a *journey*. This is a time-honored adage: "It's a marathon, not a sprint." It doesn't happen overnight like that. Success is a process by which you gradually become better, a process by which you evolve, by which you become someone who is knowledgeable and wise, pursuing everything the right way.

Success is not an event. Success is a process every time. You don't just all of the sudden have success. It is a process towards success, and to working towards goals to making yourself as successful as you possibly can. That is all a process; not an event.

SO HOW DO I TURN IT FROM A HOBBY TO A BUSINESS?

There seems to be this illusion that people refer to as "my big break." I'd like to dispel that myth and burst that bubble right from the start. Having a book go viral, having it adapted into a screenplay, having your story touch others' lives: that's success. And that doesn't happen overnight. It is a *process*.

In fact, one of the secrets in that process of trying to sell books? *Write more books.* Seriously! One of the best ways to sell books is to write more books, especially in a series.

So, get the "big break" mentality out of your mind from the very beginning. Focus on building and on construction in this first phase, because you don't just *break into* writing success; you build and you get there, eventually. The business comes first, then your craft. You form a solid foundation for whatever craft you decide to pursue, or whatever vocation you choose to pursue, not the other way around.

You have to have a foundation in order for the craft to grow and to thrive. Looking at it another way, you have to have a vehicle to take your craft somewhere. That foundation and that vehicle is the structure of a business. Build your foundation first, and then build on that foundation.

There are five questions that you should ask yourself if you want to be successful in any entrepreneurial pursuit. Here they are:

Who are you? What makes you *you*?

What uniqueness do you bring to the table? Why should someone choose you over someone else? What attracts a reader to you as opposed to another author?

What makes you not just unique, but *better*? What makes you better for this job than all the *hordes* of other authors that are out there? What do you represent where they would say, "Well, there's all these guys, but then there's Aaron Ryan…I'll buy *his* books, thankyouverymuch!"

What did you *used* to do? Or what do you do now that you never want to do again? For me, that was wedding videography. Is there something that you do as a vocation, as a breadwinner? Something that provides for you that you just don't want to do anymore? This is an entrepreneurial question. If you're trapped in a non-entrepreneurial pursuit, working for someone else's dream, you have to identify that and systematically plan to step away from it and make that crossover into writing.

Speaking of leap, are you prepared to *sacrifice* for your writing dream? One thing I'll talk about in this chapter and in other chapters is that you have to develop a mentality of expenses as *investments*. There are things that I bought that I did not consider as an "Okay, if I must" type of purchase. They were critical. My thoughts were, "I *must* have this for my future success. It is *critical* that I have this". Are you prepared to sacrifice for your dream?

If you have not had mentoring as an author, you need to stop what you're doing. Put this book down, or take it back to the clerk and ask for a refund. (Kidding. Don't do that please.) Go back to the drawing board and get mentoring.

Now, I'm not a mentor, and I'm not going to sell you on a mentoring package and ask you to enter your credit card number here. That's not who I am. But it is highly recommended that you get mentoring to know how to find your target genre, how to understand how the industry works, how to become a better writer, etc. (You *can* pursue multiple writing genres by the way: that just shows your diversity.) You need a mentor to help you learn how to write and market and get yourself out there well, *and* to develop thick skin for the rejection you'll face. Some days you'll sell hundreds of books. Others you'll sell one. Some days you may have a goose egg.

These are hard truths, but you must accept them, and a mentor can help you prepare for that.

Mentoring will help refine your already God-given writing ability into something that's compelling, something that is mysterious, deep, powerful, full and rich, and *believable*. A mentor helps you do that.

Remember this?

Mentoring > Knowledge > Application > Promotion

You start with mentoring, you move on to amassing knowledge, then you apply it, then you start promoting yourself and your books. Once you've got those tools in your toolkit – mentoring and knowledge – *then* you start applying it and then reaching out and sharing with the world what you have written.

I'm going to highly recommend a book that is not part of the "authoring booksphere". It is called 'The E-Myth" by Michael Gerber. And it talks about three different roles that are indispensable for you in running a VO business, or any business. But as a writing business, it is essential that you employ all three of these roles. Now, you can outsource some of these things, sure. But you can never outsource the technician side of it. *You* are the one who is performing the work.

The three roles are technician, manager, entrepreneur.

The technician is the person who does the work. The manager is the one who runs the business. The entrepreneur is the one who has the vision for the future, and who lays the groundwork for growth, for prosperity, for a business plan of attack, for a mission statement, and for a mantra.

The E-Myth is such an excellent book! It is *loaded* with all kinds of insight as to why each role is critical. Again, yes, you can outsource, say, your marketing, to someone else. But unless you have a stake in *how* that marketing is done, then it's really not yours anymore. It belongs to someone else. You'd be outsourcing a very important component that allows you *personally* to connect with people, not someone else saying "Aaron Ryan is great". It's *you* saying, "Hi, I do writing and I love it. And I'd love to show you my book."

Get that book – I highly recommend it. Learn those three roles that will help you in your writing business.

A MANTRA FOR ANY ENTREPRENEUR

A business mantra is so essential for understanding who you are, what you offer, why you do what you do, and where you want to go. My mantra is something that unfortunately comes from one of the Star Wars movies that I like to pretend does not exist: *The Phantom Menace*. I just wish it would go away. It is *so* not part of my Star Wars canon. Be that as it may, the mantra is uttered by Qui Gon Jinn to a young Anakin Skywalker. He says the following:

> *Your focus determines your reality.*

My friend, that is a powerful phrase, in any pursuit!

Remember Michael Phelps, professional Olympian swimmer? That man is made of steel! How many hours did he log in the pool prior to the Olympics? How many records and medals did he take home? His focus determined his reality. All the pioneers in history: their focus determined their reality.

> **Good is always the worst enemy of best.**

Make writing your *focus*; become intent beyond any measure to make this a success. Tell yourself: I'm going to focus, I'm going to learn, I'm going to grow, I'm going to market, I'm going to brand, I'm going to practice, I'm going to get mentoring, I'm going to take group mentoring and teaching and refine my skills. I'm going to learn about how to run a writing business professionally. *Your focus determines your reality.* Never forget that.

A mission statement is an excellent thing to have as well: to define your business and your pursuits that way, their reasons for doing what you do and how you do it. Very important from the start to have that. What things do you need to start your writing business and to actually treat it like a business? Where do you want to go? What do you want to be known for?

Here's my mission statement:

> ***Aaron Ryan is dedicated to the utmost quality of authoring in tandem with encouragement,***

affirmation, and works that inspire, entertain, and motivate.

ALL KINDS OF BUSINESS TIPS

I've got a long list of random business tips that I'm going to run through. These are things that have been formative for me, and instrumental in my own success over the years. But the number one thing beyond anything else, and the foundation for being successful in anything? *Gratitude*. An attitude of gratitude.

If you were a fly on the wall in my office, every time I sell a book and I receive a notification through the KDP Champ app[15] (which is indispensible, by the way!), you will hear me say, "Thank You, Lord." I will say that every single time. Every time some reader writes and says, "I LOVED your book!": "Thank you." An attitude of gratitude. Whomever you want to thank is entirely up to you. But that attitude of gratitude lays the foundation for future success.

What comes around goes around! Call it *The Secret*: that phenomenon you saw on Oprah many years ago, whatever it is, whatever you're putting out there into the universe, back to God, however you're doing it: gratitude goes an incredibly long way towards having you reap a positive emotional and financial bounty in running your business.

Another thing that is indispensible is *intention*, not hope; intention trounces hope every time. There's a little printout on the outside of my studio door that says, "I've already been awarded all of these jobs." It's just a little phrase I have on my door that I see which puts me in a mindset of coming in, to conquer, to do well, to give it my all every time I'm going to write these books, that doesn't just pertain to writing book drafts. It pertains to everything I do in business. I *intend* to succeed, I *intend* to buy this. I *intend* to accomplish these goals. Intention trounces hope! Don't tell yourself "I *hope* maybe I'll be a success one day, God permitting." That's wishful thinking, and there's nothing wrong with that in and of itself, but you need to have *intention* to see it take root and be grounded in that. Think "I *will* get this job."

Get a logo made! A logo gives you vision for who you are, and is part of your branding. A logo shows people what you stand for. I want people to see my little AR logo, the same way they see the Nike swish, or the McDonald's "M", or the Apple symbol; just like they see the three pinnacles for Adidas.

A logo says what you're about. I'll cover branding in another chapter, but branding is basically saying what sets you apart. How do people remember who you are? And what are you really all about? Branding encapsulates who you are. It's a statement. For me it is the mission statement I shared previously. That's my branding. That is who I am. That's what I give. That's what people can expect of me. You'll want to have business cards and everything else reflect that.

Equipment! Don't cut corners here. Don't get a computer that's going to crap out on you or fail in a year. And do NOT write without some kind of local or cloud backup. Preferably both! I have had that happen. Don't be chintzy and get something cheap…just because it's cheap!

Good is always the worst enemy of best.

Don't get good. Get best. Spend a little extra to reach that higher tier of quality. Invest in yourself. If you can afford one computer, buy the one just *above* it that's a little bit more expensive. If you can afford that, buy the one just above *that* that's a little bit more expensive. Push yourself to get a higher-tier, better-quality computer. There's a reason why these are expensive. You do get what you pay for. Push yourself to get a good cloud backup service. Push yourself to get great software. Do you want to graphic design your own covers someday, maybe? Get a computer that will handle it. Do you want to record and produce your own social media videos to attract your audience? You'll need something that can handle that, especially if you're filming/editing with 4K material. That is what the big boys play with. Push yourself for things that you'll *need* for business.

You need stationery, you need something across the top of a Word document that says your name, your contact information etc. That stationery shows that you're a professional, it's not just a blank Word document with typed-in contact info.

You want a website? Sure, you can get something for free through Wix or Weebly or some other free software called WYSIWYG design ("What you see is what you get") where you just drag-and-drop in different elements. But you'll see at the bottom of all of those websites, "created by Wix", "created by Weebly", *whatever*, and then you're advertising *Wix or Weebly*; you're not advertising you. My website is authoraaronryan.com: it is a WordPress-based website. And there are no other advertisements on there! That's the way I want it. That's the way I need it. Keep them there. Don't give them any reason to be distracted and jump to the *next* author.

Get a domain that is completely *your own* domain. And get an email address that has your domain in it. Why settle for free? For example, authorrob@gmail.com, or suzywritesthings@gmail.com. Don't settle for those! Get your own personalized domain. And get suzy@suzywritesthings.com. Get me@authorrob.com. Why do you think I went ahead and setup my email to be me@authoraaronryan.com? Get a branded email to go with your website. It all looks so much more professional.

If you're looking for a great web designer that is low-cost, with excellent SEO-friendly design, check with

Chris Cummings and IWD at chris@iwdonline.com. He is fast, efficient, and cost-effective.

Cognito forms are free forms that you can sign up for if you don't know how to create a contact form on your website. Perhaps the GoDaddy/hosting or WordPress widgets don't work very well, or they're failing to reliably send you the results for some reason. You can go to Cognito forms online and create free plugin forms where you can simply grab the WordPress code and paste it into your website code. You'll see that I have one of these on my website at https://authoraaronryan.com/contact/. They work perfectly, fluidly, and they store all the results. They are excellent, free, and very customizable.

There are ways to advertise when you're mobile. You can get custom apparel: I have all kinds of different shirts that say things about authoring - and people ask questions about them! They are funny! They make people laugh. Why not? Why not spread joy and humor, and invite conversation?

I also have a vehicle that has vinyl lettering on the back window. Why not? What if I'm driving along and someone sees *"The war is coming. Visit getthesebooks.com."* (I seriously have that domain, and it forwards to https://www.dissonancetheseries.com.) If they happen to be an avid reader, and I don't have vinyl lettering on my car, I've missed an opportunity right there on the highway. If there is a reader who needs a good book, and I'm driving by (hopefully safely), I would rather have it on my vehicle than not. It also helps to deduct mileage and depreciation on your vehicle as a business expense, because you're using your vehicle for business. Get vinyl lettering. Believe in yourself. If you're an author, tell people about it.

One invaluable tool that I've discovered not a lot of people take advantage of is a disposable phone number. I use the "Burner" app for iPhone. I have a subscription for three disposable phone numbers. If a call comes in on my phone, and it's a potential reader, I know that they're calling Aaron Ryan, I know that they're calling in regards to business, that it's not just a personal call. I don't want to pick up my phone and say a casual "Hello?" if it's a reader. If they're calling Aaron Ryan, I don't want to say "Hey, what's up, this is Aaron." No. I want to say "Aaron Ryan, may I help you?"

Burner is a great app to be able to help you determine which calls are business and which calls are personal. It's a marginal nominal subscription fee that you pay monthly or yearly. But it also protects your personal cell phone number so you're not throwing that out into cyberspace and then enabling everybody and their mother to have it. You might get a really nice vanity number that just sounds great! You don't want that out there in cyberspace; get a protective, masked disposable number that people will associate with you. You might even luck into a number with seven digits such as AUTHOR1. You put *that* number on all your stationery, website, business cards, everything. That way it protects your personal cell.

Post sample excerpts of your books on Medium! Share them as articles on LinkedIn! All great exposure with great audiences to find you and your works, and then slake their thirst for more. *ALWAYS* list your URL to drive traffic to your author website.

Have Cliff's Notes versions of your books produced. Get those done to giveaway at trade shows and craft fairs so that you're not cutting into your inventory. These low-cost books are great to share with people if, say, you have a spin wheel and they've won a prize. Now you can give them a small book as a prize, and that might lead to more book purchases.

Uptime Robot[16] is a tool that I've used for my websites over the years. It's a free service. You program in your website. Anytime your site goes offline, Uptime Robot will email you. I want my sites to be online 24-7. It's unrealistic to expect that they will *never* go down, but I want them to be up as much as possible. I don't want people going to my site and seeing a 404 error. I don't want them seeing something that wards them away to the next author. I want them to stay right on my site. Uptime Robot is a great tool to let me know if something is amiss with my hosting.

This next one is absolutely critical beyond any other tip. *You must have goals.* Invisible goals are no goals at all. You need a daily goals checklist. A goals checklist will help you stay on top of your marketing, your other advertising, how many words you type per day, how many industry contacts you've made, have you done your daily social media posts, etc.. Did you reach out to marketing contacts today? Check. Are you working on a book? Check. Did you work on a chapter today? Check. Did you write your blog for the week? Check. It's totally customizable. You put your goals in there, and you track them on a daily, weekly, or monthly basis.

Make those SMART goals visible to you. You may have seen the acronym for SMART goals:

- S-pecific
- M-easurable
- A-chievable
- R-ealistic
- T-ime-bound

Have those goals visible so that you can actually see them and accomplish them; not some ethereal haze floating out there where you're thinking "what were my goals again?" No. You want to know what your goals are every day, all the time, so that you can keep track of them and accomplish them. Also, bonus! I once heard a *great* suggestion to add an -er to the end of your SMART goals. Make them smart*ER*! Not just specific, measurable, achievable, realistic, and time bound but adding an -er on the end, and making them more *E*xciting and *R*ewarding. Why not have smartER goals?

I have goals that I track every single day. If I'm not writing, blogging, or checking sales metrics, you'll find me marketing. I am a marketer (actually, an *enthusiast!*) first, and then I am an author. That marketing is part and parcel of being a business owner. In order to put my product out there I need to market. Keep track of what you're doing with marketing. Make it a goal to market and fulfill tasks each day.

Another thing that I do every day is I post an interesting post on social media. Now, when I first started doing that, they were memes or infographics. They were comical, incorporating lots of pop culture references, because I'm kind of a geek that way, and that's part of what makes me unique. Those faciliate interest! You do have to be careful to steer clear of them appearing too "advertisy" – make sure that you're not bombarding people with ads in addition to the score of them they *already* see online.

Are you looking for a writing job somewhere? A tool that I'm really fond of is the SearchTempest.com tool. SearchTempest is a site that will help you scour all of Craigslist in the jobs or gigs category. You basically search for *authoring* or *authors* or *writers*, whatever. You can program variables so it will search for different strings on all of Craigslist, not just a single city - because you can do that on Craigslist itself easily enough. SearchTempest will scour all of Craigslist, every city all over the planet for anything that is a writing job and return those results to you. I love SearchTempest because I can see all the results in one place and find jobs on Craigslist. They do exist! Some of them do not pay well; some of them do. SearchTempest is a great tool.

Another one of my goals every day is to follow five to ten authors, literary agents, publishers, etc., on Twitter. I like building those associations. I like following people and seeing what they're up to. I also like following my readers, letting them know that I'm here, and conversing with them on social media. You can actually even score book purchsaes by following the right people on Twitter who are looking for books to read and buy.

I once knew a voice talent who is very social on LinkedIn in particular. She posts engaging content that draws in readers and colleagues. You need to interact with those readers and be a *human* with them. Humans like humans! Have human contact with these people, and *engage* with them on social media. You do that by reading their stories, posting your own stories and asking questions, sharing articles, getting people to interact and engage with you. That's how you develop a following and an audience. And that's how people remember you and follow you. Don't be "that guy" who is always posting ad-like content. We see enough ads already. Don't be shallow. Be a real human.

Another of my goals every day is to work on my weekly blog. I usually release a new blog every week or few weeks: they are inspirational, comical, celebratory, and motivating for me to write.

People ask me often: "how do you have time to do all that marketing?" The answer is simple. I do not "have" time - I *make* time. Now, am I some almighty being who is capable of expanding our 24 hours into 28 per day? No. I neither have nor want such power.

In the 24 hours that *are* allotted to me, and the eight to ten that are allotted for work, specifically, *I* choose what I want to do with those hours; it's up to *me* to choose what to do with that time. And I choose to be enthusiastic about writing and about what I've written. I want others to catch that enthusiasm.

Ultimately, my job is to be able to put "irons in the fire" out there to feed that pipeline; to connect with readers; to keep things coming back to me. Everything I throw out there is a boomerang. I want those boomerangs to come loaded. I want them to bring back readers and buyers, etc.

I want them to bring back contacts, interests, and communications. I want readers to say, "Sure, send me to your author website." I want that to return to me a good return on investment (ROI).

For my efforts to make a return on investment, I want to get those marketing outreaches done every day. My business utterly depends on this.

So again - do I have time? No, I *make* time because I want my writing business to be a success. You need to adopt the same principle if you want your business to be a success, and really employ that marketing every day. Make time for it.

HUSTLE

I'm going to give you an acronym that has never been heard before. I made it myself. Soon this will be repeated everywhere and I'll be called *genius*.

It's called *hustle*. It's six letters, and I'm going to break it down for you. Hustle is so critical to your success not just as an author, but in life.

Many times when I post marketing content or try to connect with literary agents online, with someone I've never talked to before, I've actually gotten a reply back that said, "Great work, Aaron. I appreciate the hustle." I mean, *wow*! They've appreciated that I've contacted them. They appreciate that it is, in fact, a hustle: that I'm trying to get myself out there.

- The H stands for *hungry*. You have to stay hungry in order to put food on your table. You have to stay hungry for work. Keep that hunger - H is hungry.
- U is *undeterred*. The fact is that you're going to get some people that don't want you to contact them and say "take me off your list right now." You cannot be deterred by these people. They're just angry grumps, or they'e had a bad day. The next person, or the next-next-next person will inevitably say "thank you for emailing. Sure, I'll put you on my roster." Be undeterred in the face of resistance.
- S is *strategic*. Be strategic with your hustle. Don't just throw craziness all over the universe and hope that something sticks. Be *methodical*, be *systematic*, be *professional* in your hustle; be *strategic* in how you put your marketing out there with people. This also pertains to business as well. Be strategic in how you run your writing business.

- Be *tenacious*. Don't give up. This is an everyday a week thing. It's a 24/7 pursuit. This hustle is 24/7. Keep feeding that pipeline. Be tenacious with it.
- L - *living the dream*. You are living the dream as an author. This is such a dream career! You get to *create* all the time! I pinch myself every day that I get to do this, and some days I wake up laughing. It is a *dream*. Live this dream that's part of your hustle.
- The E is *endless*; it never ends. You don't ever stop hustling as an author; you don't just coast and rest on your laurels. It doesn't just kind of become this commission bounty, and these royalties and residuals just stream in all over you. It's a constant hustle – endless – until Jesus returns. You have to develop a long-term vision in order to understand the endless nature of hustle, and sustain that vision.

OTHER TIPS

You may have heard of the concept of duplication: this goes back a little bit to mentoring. You receive what others instruct, you learn it, and duplicate it. Why people want to reinvent the wheel is beyond me. You've heard the phrase "if it ain't broke, don't fix it." Duplication spares you from reinventing the wheel.

Follow those who have gone before, and adapt it to your own style, your own flavor, your own taste, but *duplicate* these people. There's a reason they're successful. This is really why you get mentoring, and why you skip mentoring to your own peril. These people have done it. These people are *doing* it.

Don't. Skip. Mentoring.

Duplicate those people that are successful, emulate them, take what they do, do it for yourself. Duplication works. Take their chocolate-chip cookie recipe and, what the heck, maybe throw almonds in it. It's still a chocolate-chip cookie recipe that you duplicated and built upon. And *everyone* likes chocolate-chip cookies. Imitation is the purest form of flattery.

I never once saw writing as a *hobby*. I never once treated it that way. When I discovered what I had, I *knew* this was it. It was always a business venture. For me, it made absolute sense because it makes use of all of my giftings: creativity, organization, empathy-giving, performance, business acumen, and more.

We all have different makeup. Some of us may underachieve in one area, or perhaps overachieve in another. Bottom line is: treat this like a business, never a hobby. Use all of your gifts. Look at this industry and this vocation, and say, "Is this making use of all of my gifts?" If so, you're going to succeed. If not, find out what gifts are that you might be lacking, and get training in order to *develop* those gifts. Build them up so that you can succeed and be well-rounded in this industry.

SUSTAINING A THRIVING WRITING BUSINESS

Now - how do we *sustain* a thriving writing business? How do we actually keep this thing called authoring going every day? How do we grease the wheel in order to see this continue to rotate and produce results and take us places? I'm going to go through a list here of just a bunch of different things, as before.

Aside from the obvious of forming a Facebook page for reviews, or gathering reviews left for your books on Amazon or Goodreads, you can form a Yelp page or a Google Local page. Ask for reviews from readers there! Seriously! Reviews anywhere tell prospective readers that current or past readers liked you. Get reviews as often as you can, and everywhere you can. Be shameless about that. Try to recruit those reviews to build up your page and your reputation, so that people can find you on Google, Facebook, Yelp, LinkedIn, wherever. Recruit those endorsements and recommendations on LinkedIn. They're invaluable. Get those, because that's no longer *you* talking about how good you are. I hate tooting my own horn that way. It's other people doing that PR work for you! There's nothing better. A good word is better than great riches.

Learn to say *no*. There are a lot of things that will come at you in your business, such as ways to try this or do that or help this person or that person, AKA, "get sidetracked." *No is your favorite Yes*. Learn to say no, because that's saying *yes* to you. Your time is your most valuable commodity. Don't let these "time sucks" come along and bleed you dry. There are people who are walking umbilical cords and they'll plug right into you and they'll just drain you dry. You don't want that - steer clear of that. Learn to say no to distractions i.e., too much scrolling through news feeds on social media, playing games like *Bejeweled* or *Candy Crush* or whatever else, and other distractions on your computer. There's marketing that you can do. There's learning that you can do. There's practice that you can do. There's research you can do. *No.*

Never overpromise and underdeliver. Do the opposite. I love Scotty (Mr. Scott) in Star Trek 3. Captain Kirk asked him about his repair estimate. Scotty said "it will take eight weeks, sir - but you don't have eight weeks so I'll do it for ya in two." And Kirk says "Mr. Scott, have you always multiplied your repair estimates by a factor of four?" And Scotty said, "of course! How else can I keep my reputation as a miracle worker?" I love that! Don't overpromise people on your books, such as with false premises in the title, subtitle, log line or description. Don't promise them unrealizable release dates. Instead, *under*-promise and *over*-deliver. Does that make sense? That way people are *pleasantly surprised* when you deliver quickly and correctly. They're surprised when you respond right away. Unfortunately, this is a huge trap that a lot of business owners fall prey to, because they want to get work - and I do understand that. Authors are the same, because we want to get buying readers. Don't surrender to that mentality. Keep your wits about you. Underpromise, be rational, reasonable, and then overdeliver.

Don't obsess over whether you've been given a high rating or a review on any site your book is listed on. If you get a four-star out of a five-star review, who cares? If you get a three-star, reflect on what you could have done better, if you're afforded that possibility. But if you ever get a no-response or a low response, don't hang your hat on that: you can't steer your life by the rearview mirror. You have to keep moving forward. Let the low reviews go. Accept them as teaching instruments, and then let them go. *You cannot please everyone, nor should you try. That is futile.* Don't wait with baited breath over whether or not someone liked your book. Don't stew over whether or not someone is going to buy your book. You're better than that. Keep moving forward. Keep planting seeds. Keep writing good books.

I'm not going to go too heavily into this but if you don't have a smartphone, you're living in the past. Get a smartphone. You can use a voice memo recorder on your phone to help you record ideas when you're out, and stay on top of things by checking the memos when you get home. You can take notes when you're out, and remind yourself to take care of items when you arrive home, such as geo-fenced reminders. When I'm out getting groceries, I can ask Siri to "remind me to email Barbara when I get home and tell her 'thank you so much for the kind review.'" Siri is great about that. And Alexa and other such devices, they're all great for keeping you on top of things like that.

Keyboard shortcuts on your phone save you *so* much time from typing the same exact thing over and over again. If you're marketing to people, use the same text and change the name, and then personalize it some more. But if the overall message remains the same, program that into your phone so you can use a keyboard shortcut to invoke it and not have to type up the same marketing message to everyoen every single time.

Email signature: In your signature on your smartphone, you can put all your social media links (or LinkTree or Dot Cards profile) and your website link. You want to direct potential readers to your author website and available books, don't you?

Everywhere you can, as much as it depends on you, list your writing website for a quality backlink from whatever website you're on. If you're posting something in a forum somewhere, as long as you're not in violation of the rules, list your website, because Google will see that website pointing back to you. It's called a quality backlink. Google likes those.

KEEP UP THAT MARKETING

I'm going to talk about marketing at length soon. But for a preview, know a few things as they pertain to business:

Marketing is not 80/20. It really is like 95/5. You're marketing *all the time*, every day. You have to develop a flavor, and a taste, and a penchant, and a *commitment* to that. If you're going to succeed as a business owner who writes – or *any* business owner – you have to drive traffic to yourself.

You should follow up with your leads in marketing, such as with local bookstores you've asked to carry your books, or to inquire how they're selling.

You'll want to program Outlook or calendar reminders to follow up with people at regular intervals. Ask them how they're selling. Ask them did they get everything they needed? It's amazing how many times I've gotten a book sale, or a new batch book order, simply because out of the blue, I asked how readers or buyers were doing right at that moment. That goes a really long way: reaching out to readers and buyers and saying, "How are you? How are you doing? Is everything okay?" "How are you doing?" goes a long way. And then you're back on their radar again, and they say "you know what? Aaron really cares! I can tell he really cares about how I'm doing. I'm going to buy some more books from him to sell in our store." Love it! I love when they do that.

Is it manipulative? No. Do I genuinely care how my readers are doing? Yes. I have a reader in Florida who was set to get married during in 2020, and then the pandemic happened. They called it off, not because they fell out of love with each other, but because it just wasn't the right timing. I care about her. She's purchased my book and kept in touch, and I consider her a friend.

These readers and buyers are your friends: many of them. So do what you need to do to treat them as friends and as human beings - and make sure that they know you care. Send them gift cards. Send them holiday greeting cards. Thank them. Keep yourself on their radar by being involved in their lives. Your relationship with them doesn't have to be solely about authoring. Get to know their story too.

Marketing is so critical to putting bread on your table and continuing to share about your business. It's not something that everybody likes, I get it. But you have to do it if you want to survive as a business owner: you have to be willing to toot your own horn. You have to be willing to reach out and connect with people and tell them what you do. Vinyl lettering isn't enough. Wearing custom branded apparel isn't enough; having business cards isn't enough. You have to hand them out. You have to tell people who you are. You have to put yourself out there. That takes bravery, but so did writing your book. You are brave. Go forth bravely.

Trade shows, craft fairs and vendor markets are a great way of marketing. Get out there! Meet people. Attend these events with readers and buyers! Get out and meet those people! Tell them what you do. Share with them enthusiastically about what you wrote. Have conversations, be real, be a human, talk about what you wrote and get the word out that way, while finding out more about them in the same stretch.

YOUR DAY TO DAY

Let's talk about daily structure. Make sure to structure your day clearly. Develop a plan of attack and settle into a routine. This again goes back to having a trackable goals system so that you can monitor your progress throughout the day, week, or month, and get into a system of marketing - and *adhere* to it every day. If you want to carve out an hour, a half hour, or even 15 minutes, make sure you have a daily schedule with reminders that pop up that tell you to do what you need to do. There's no shame in having these reminders. I've committed so much of my memory to my voice memo app, to my Outlook calendar, and to Siri, that I'm sure I'll end up with dementia and a bad case of drool. Ha! I've just done so much offloading of what I need to do that now it's all there to remind me, and I don't have to remember anymore. The computers and the technology are there for a reason. Use them, even if you'll end up a drooling freak by age 40.

Make sure there is an allocation of time not only to market, but especially to write. Keep writing! Write on!

If you don't blog, I want to ask why. Start blogging! It does not necessarily have to be about writing; it can be about your life. Your blogs should be about 500 words minimum each – and content-rich. Google loves content-rich websites and blogs that have traffic to them, and where Google can recognize you as an *authority* on a subject. Google looks at me as an authority on the subject of writing. Because I blog regularly, because I have traffic, because I have outbound links to other websites, and they link back to me in some cases, Google sees me as an authority. All search engines like sites that are active, and that have heavy content with keyword-rich blogs. They can be about whatever you want them to be. But they do show Google that you have an active site. Start blogging.

Reply *quickly*. Readers and buyers love it when they don't have to wait. They love quick responses. They love getting answers to what they want. Don't you? Aren't we all the same? I don't know about you, but when I fire off a few inquiries to a contractor on Craigslist, the one who replies first is the one who gets my prime consideration; the one who replies week later and apologizes for their late reply won't even get a second thought from me; it's quite possible the job has already been done, anyway.

In the same light, your potential buyer didn't ask a question so they could wait a few days for the answer, right? They need their answers now. The quicker you can reply, the better. I've been complimented here and there by buyers who joked that they received an answer to their question *before* they even sent their question. Reply quickly, and impress your buyers in so doing.

You should also have software such as an office suite: preferably, Microsoft Office or OpenOffice. You'll of course need these if you want to write. Dave Chesson with Kindlepreneur recommends Atticus software. Another great one is Vellum (for Mac only, as of this writing)[17], as well as Autocrit[18]. And of course there's Microsoft Word or Grammarly[19], although Grammarly now really heavily promotes AI integration, and that turns me off. I'll explain my distaste for AI here in a bit. There are suites of software programs that you can use to put forward professional templates and documents, contracts, invoices, letterhead, anything that you need stationery for, anything that you need to send out to readers that has your contact info on it. You need something good, preferably something that you've invested in, that you can use to put forward a professional appearance. Plain text documents and in-email text-only proposals don't cut it anymore. Use office suites that help you *look* professional and *be* professional.

Digital organization: use logic! Use file folders and subfolders for your readers. If a reader has booked you, make a folder. If they booked you again, then you need to separate their folder into two sub-folders. For example:

- Name of your book
    - Subfolder for Kindle version
    - Subfolder for Cover Artwork
    - Subfolder for Drafts
- Name of other book
    - Subfolder, so on and so forth

It is *critical* to remain organized. Organization is the BFF to a business owner. It's your best friend. Organization on your hard desktop of your desk, removing clutter, and organizing your Windows or MacOS desktop are important. Reduce the clutter in your life. Find your BFF.

I suggest using two different browsers: one for business, and one for personal. That way you don't convolute your messages. That way, you're not responding to a reader as a family member. That way, you're not posting something political, and one of your readers see it. That way, you're not bombarding your family with a bunch of advertisements and posts that deal with your business, rather than sharing foodies. I use Chrome in one monitor for my business, and I use Opera in another browser for my personal stuff. I keep that separation. That way I don't mix and match the two accidentally. Foodies and politics don't mix well with readers.

There are plenty of Facebook groups that you can join. I highly recommend joining the Self-Publishing Support group on Facebook at https://www.facebook.com/groups/706924932809745: it's a great group. You can connect with myriad colleagues that way. There are several others. In the business of authoring, there are plenty of groups on Facebook, and LinkedIn as well. Learn from people who've gone before. Learn from people who are on the same career trajectory that you are on; ask questions; learn together. Grow together. These networking groups are indispensable, and there is no shortage in this day and age of online networking resources for us to be able to learn and grow together.

The way that I track if my marketing is working is if I actually pay attention to the aforementioned KDP Champ app, and my sales metrics on KDP and Ingram Spark and Draft2Digital. They all send reports to me as well. If I'm getting a bunch of purchases, that means my marketing is working. That means people are seeing my email or my promotions, responding to my email, going to the website for whatever book they're interested in, and purchasing. It does tell me a lot about my ROI.

You're never done learning. The day you stop learning is the day you're room temperature…and the day you die. You always have to learn and grow, because trends change in the writing industry. Presentations change, marketing tactics change, tendencies change, and advertising styles change. The way you read changes. Please: *never stop learning.*

Return to mentoring, return to groups, return to conferences, return to reading. The best way to connect with your readers is by continuing to read, yourself. Keep yourself sharp and informed. It's just so critical. You have to continue to grow. I think the phrase was "grapes grow best in bunches." I'll talk about that a bit more here coming up. The more that you can associate with colleagues who can teach you, or with mentors who can teach you, then you're going to be a really rich, delicious, succulent grape. Or…something.

Always be grateful. Always proceed in gratitude. Never forget the first reader who bought a book from you.

Good is always the worst enemy of best. Good is settling for. Best is striving towards the ultimate. Best is *alive*. It's functional. It's success-building. Choose best. Never settle for good, or for "good enough." Choose best. You *can* do this. You *can* do writing as a career. Make *best* choices as you do it.

I highly encourage you to treat it like a business: to take the steps necessary to invest in your business, to learn to grow, to buy the right things, to get the mentoring, to treat it like a business so that you actually have something tangible where you can look back and say, "I am *so* glad I never treated this like a hobby and shortchanged myself in the process."

One more time for good measure: You absolutely *can* do this as a solid business that provides for you and your family.

Ready? It's time to start.

CHAPTER 4: MARKETING & VISIBILITY FOR YOUR WRITING BUSINESS

YOU ARE A MARKETER

Actually, no you're not. You're an *enthusiast.* That is the most important thing you can be. After all, no one will ever be as enthusiastic about what you write…as you! Marketing and enthusiasm are very strong passions of mine. I'm humbled to have a voice, this God-given voice, and this ability to articulate it through my fingers into print. We all have it! It is absolutely amazing what we get to do with this creativity of ours, these fingers of ours, and with this intellect of ours, and the abilities to dream, to market, to promote, to utterly believe in what we're doing. To make ourselves a success doing something we love. Marketing, and being an enthusiast, allows us to get that God-given gift out there.

Again, "find what you love to do, you'll never work a day in your life." It's so very true. I don't *work* a day in my life, because I love what I do.

Now, let's talk about branding for a minute. We're going to talk about social media visibility – and in that, branding is very important.

I enjoyed the movie *Batman Begins* with Christian Bale. There's one scene where Christian Bale's Bruce Wayne is on a plane with Alfred The Butler, and he's says the following:

People need dramatic examples to shake them out of apathy and I can't do that as Bruce Wayne. As a man, I'm flesh and blood, I can be ignored, I can be destroyed; but as a symbol... as a symbol I can be incorruptible, I can be everlasting.

I'd like to encourage you from the very start: stop being only a person. You are no longer just a person, you are now a *persona*. A persona is represented by a symbol.

When you start looking at yourself as a *persona*, then you start moving more into the territory of being like the Nike Swish, like the McDonald's "M", like the three pinnacles of Adidas, like the Apple logo. When you stop looking at yourself merely as a person and start looking at yourself as a *persona*, you become more of a contender in the writing sphere, in terms of selling power, in terms of respectability, in terms of marketing, in terms of not just participation, but really making a difference.

My brand tagline while as a voiceover artist was *Super human being · Superhuman voice.* I gave a lot in the authoring community, thus the first part of my branding:

- I ran The Voices In My Head Blog.

- I ran the Global Authors Network Facebook group.
- I wrote a book series to encourage - I love to encourage! It just brings some laughter. It's a joy, and a fresh focus. It's still available on Amazon under my former stage name, Josh Alexander.[20]
- I wrote a voiceover book similar to this one.
- I taught for free in webinars and online conferences.
- I reviewed colleagues' demos for free.
- I shared marketing tips and goals worksheets with those who ask.
- I occasionally gave my books and training courses away.
- I provided 20-minute authoring video consults free of charge to aspiring authors all the time, to encourage you to know and to awaken to the knowledge that you can actually do this as a business.

The first part is the giving side of it. I wanted to be a reflection of the generosity that was sown into me. The *superhuman voice* is because I have a dynamic and diverse voice, different accents, British, Australian, Caribbean, Mexican, old, young, different styles and timbers and cadences, etc., and I wanted to offer a wide palette of vocal range.

So that's where my tagline came from for voiceovers. And that makes me more of a persona.

For authoring, I want people to see my logo I shared earlier, and think "Oh hey, that's Aaron Ryan!" It's a name recognition thing. It's an image recognition. It's something that you want to leave people with that they will always remember.

For me, I'm marketing all day long. I'm turning over rocks. It's the thrill of the hunt. It's trying to find the next potential reader and to really conduct that outreach all day long.

Marketing isn't for everyone. Not everyone likes it. I really do. In some respects, I have a very shameless approach towards getting my services out there. You do have to be shameless in the promotion of your business, for you to survive and to be a contender in the writing marketplace, to offer something of value, and help people to see that what you're offering is in fact *in-valuable.* It takes a bit of an aggressive edge to continue putting yourself out there.

I'd like to share a section from my book, "*Voiceovers: A Super Business · A Super Life.*" It's from a chapter called "The Thrill of the Hunt." The section talks about how the marketing aspect is really about the hunt. Not so much the acquisition, but the hunt:

"The lioness stalks its prey with stealth. Slowly creeping through the tall reeds, it eyes its wildebeest prize, that great mound of juicy flesh...that succulent payoff. But ultimately, the lioness has something far greater in mind than the final meal. It's not the payoff, really. Rather, it's the moment the wildebeest becomes aware of her, muscles flex, joints spring into action, and the wildebeest blows out of there like a tornado, desperate to evade the predator. That is when life happens for the lioness... for the jaguar... for the cheetah... eyes widen as their prey takes off...*and the chase is on.*"

I wrote that in my best movie trailer voice.

That's really what this is all about everyday: looking, looking, looking and finding someone - and then the connection! That's the fruit of your labors. And it's so wonderful to find buyers and readers.

But back to sowing those seeds. Remember, marketing cannot be just about the finish line. Marketing needs to be about the *love* of marketing, or you will burn out. You must communicate enthusiasm, and you must *remain* enthusiastic while doing it. It must be about tilling soil, it must be about planting seeds. It must be about reaching out. It must be about the joy of connecting. That's what marketing, and enthusiasm about what you wrote, is all about. Fred Bear said "A hunt based only on the trophies taken falls far short of what the ultimate goal should be." And I agree.

I love the phrase from Reinhold Eisner who ascended Mount Everest without supplemental oxygen in 1980. He was asked "why did you go up there to die?" He said "I didn't go up there to die. I went up there to *live*." Does marketing thrill you? If not, it's time you figure out how to make it do so.

If you adopt a new perspective, *yesterday*, post-haste, that you are not an author; you are a *marketer* who just happens to do writing, you will start to become incredibly successful. As with being a businessman first, I am also a marketer first, who just happens to write. That's why I'm successful at marketing.

Here's an approach I'd like to share in terms of marketing in my approach with readers. I use the "Ask" Approach.

- A stands for "Allowing"
- S stands for "Sensitive"
- K stands for "Kind"

Allowing: in this day and age you're allowing your reader to go about their day. I tend to prefer social media marketing via direct email. It's non-intrusive, it's not "in your face" like a phone call is. It's allowing them to answer on their time.

Sensitive is along the same wavelength but it's more about not shoving your goods and wares down their throat. Not coming across as the very best author there ever was. *"I'm the best author there is"* is arrogant. *Sensitive* is not about hubris or bravado. Go in sensitively, understanding that you are one of *many* who offer an invaluable product. I truly believe my book quadrilogy and my other offerings are invaluable. But approaching that humbly will open doors for me.

You also go in *Kindly*. Use manners. Use please and thank you. Be respectful. *Ask* if you can send a sample portion of your book. Agents and publishers will ask you for samples of what you'ev written.

I like the *ASK* approach because all of it reflects humility.

All of it also reflects the ability to leave the ball in their court. No high pressure. I'm not a high-pressure sales guy. I like to just extend the invitation, and I pretty much leave it at that. I will follow up if they've asked me to do so. I like to back off and just let them make the decision to buy my book in their own time. The same is true for me at trade shows. People love to buy. They hate to be sold.

Thomas Edison said that "genius is 1% inspiration and 99% perspiration." What a fantastic truth. You're going to be marketing a lot. Get ready to sweat a bit.

I just do it, just like Nike. I choose what my day is going to look like - *I* decide. I am in charge of my own destiny. This is my business. No one can force me to do something I don't want to do. I decide what to do with my time and my efforts and my energy and my inspiration. In my business as the business owner, I choose how to run my business. If I want mywriting business to go on, to continue, then I'm going to market my books every day. I'm going to choose to reach out to people every day.

I need irons in the fire. I need to cast a wide net. And because I need to, I *choose* to. *You* choose what your day looks like. The question is not "do I have the time or not?"

Here's a good example: I was asked to teach on voiceover marketing in 2020 for a conference in the middle of 2020's pandemic, with a four-year-old who was constantly bursting into my office for attention, and a one-year-old who wants his Dada. I'm constantly auditioning and marketing and blogging. And to top it off, we were moving to a new home in the midst of all of that. There is *SO* much to do when one is moving from one home to another. If you've moved, you know this. So I ask you, did I not have time? No, I *made* the time. I don't have a calculator handy. But if you take 24 hours times seven, that's a lot of hours! (I'm right-brained. I'm creative, so I can't multiply, ha!) But that's a *lot* of hours that you can do a *lot* with in the span of a week. The choice is really up to you what you intend to do with it.

> *I choose what my day is going to look like - I decide. I am in charge of my own destiny. This is my business. No one can force me to do something I don't want to do. I decide what to do with my time and my efforts and my energy and my inspiration.*

It's been said "work smarter; not harder." I tend to disagree a little bit with that - you do want to get to a point where you're working smarter more than harder, sure. But why can't you work smarter *and* harder? Why can't you do both? I like to do a "smarter, harder" approach. Not everyone is going to do the amount of outreaches that I do per week. And I'm not going to do the amount of outreaches that some other people do.

Some people out there might eclipse what I do. I am not as effective as some, and some are not as effective as me. However you slice it, be effective. Get to work.

Work smarter and harder. There's no reason why you can't do both. That's why I'm a success. I work smart. And I work hard. I incorporate goals and corporate tactics. I have a mission statement, I have a mantra, I am *intent* on what I'm going to do with my day. I thoroughly and utterly believe in my products.

You just do it, and you just go through with it. Don't waste your day playing games and surfing news feeds, all the while letting an entire eight hours - 480 valuable minutes - slip away from you. Maximize your day. Do that with a clear focus and goals.

So how do I actually get this done? I think after a while, just as you do with a smartphone, for example, you develop muscle memory, you flick here, you push this, you do that, you slide here, you move that over, you slide down, you develop muscle memory for a lot of things you do in your life. I'm posting across multiple social media sites. Or, *si vous plais,* you could automate and use a tool like Hootsuite, if that suits you, and hit many of them all at once.

Muscle memory is very important in marketing, particularly if you're going off of lists for emails, or performing the same task over and over in contacting new potential readers. Case in point: each day I will market to thousands of people online. Now, I am aware that there have been studies that show that you can market more effectively at a different time of the day, or specific days of the week. I tend to do more of a shotgun approach with my marketing and cast that wide net, because in some respects I believe it's a numbers game, and you have *chaos theory* at play.

What is chaos theory? Chaos is the science of surprises, of the nonlinear and the unpredictable. It teaches us to expect the unexpected.[21] Ultimately, all of our hard-conducted tests and surveys and analyses can fall flat and be subject to change. One year people can respond better on a Tuesday afternoon. The next it's Thursday morning. The next it's Sunday evening. It's relatively inconsistent. So, my solution to that is to be consistent in just doing it every day, around the same time.

I usually will market in the mid-morning and get all those done. I market one at a time. I don't do bulk "bcc" emails. I love to market via direct email. And I'll market via email through Instagram. I'll also do that via emails that come from directories, harvested emails from mailing lists that I will either assimilate myself, or I've purchased. I will customize each individual email. So, if the reader's email is rick@mulliganmedia.com, I will say "Hi, Rick!" as opposed to "Hi there!" My message is customized to that person.

I know that when I get an email from someone that says "Hi there!" Or… "Hello AARON RYAN." Come on. That message was not personalized to me. It's not customized to me. It was spit out by a mail merge program. They didn't take the time to reach out to *me* specifically. They are shooting off multiple emails rapid-fire and hoping for the best. It's untargeted. So, my muscle memory comes into play by copy > paste > change name > send...copy > paste > change name > send. Rinse and repeat. Changing their name makes it much more personalized.

It doesn't take me but probably an hour a day to do my marketing. So don't make marketing this great big scary beast and say, "I don't have time to do that." *Make* time. My daily outreaches are spread across emails, TikTok, Facebook, Pinterest, Threads, LinkedIn, Instagram, and Twitter, etc.. For the emails specifically, I am actually reaching out to those people directly.

Again, maybe an hour a day. And if I'm working an eight-hour day, I still have seven whole hours to audition and to produce and to make money and to be successful. One hour per day of marketing has reaped incredible results for me.

Did you know blogging is a form of marketing? Do you blog? If not, can you start? I'm going to refer a lot of people – as I often do – to Paul Strikwerda's blog, "Nethervoice." It has been an incredible inspiration to me in particular while as a voice talent. I love Paul's blog. There are other bloggers out there that I draw from as well.

When you blog, you're sharing content that's very important to you that has an authoring spin on it. But your blogging doesn't necessarily have to be about authoring; you can write about your life.

Blogging doesn't just serve me, though. And it doesn't just serve my audience. Blogging serves my position and my standing with Google. I talked about this in an earlier chapter. So, if you have an author website, and all you have on there is a page with your "about" info with your demos, a contact page, etc., you should setup a blog on there, even if your blog is only going to be 500 words about your current day. It can be about marketing, it can be about your family, it can be about whatever. But it is Google seeing your authoring website, active out there in cyberspace, putting out content – again, content is king. Get into the habit. It doesn't take very long.

I absolutely love the creative avenue of blogging. Start blogging. Connect with your readers who have intentionally signed up on your blog. Offer the occasional free giveaway. Get new signups at trade shows and craft fairs and vendor markets. Invite people to subscribe to your blog online.

You can use a tool like an email spider to gather leads. It's a program where you look online in, for example, a directory of readers & buyers. You grab that URL, and program it into a spider. In my case, I use Email Extractor 6. I program the domain in there, run the search, and it goes to that website and pulls down all valid email addresses that I can use in order to market to those people. An email spider is excellent for harvesting emails of potential readers. True, an email spider is a little bit controversial because I'm data mining, and some people don't like that. We live in an age where people want their privacy. I do understand that. But they are in a public directory online that I can easily harvest and contact them. Will all those emails be current and valid? Probably not. Many of them are, and I've gotten readers by doing so. Google "email spider" or Email Extractor 6 as an example, and start grabbing free emails out there.

Now, don't try to run Email Extractor 6 on Craigslist, it will get you banned. Don't try to do it on LinkedIn, Craigslist, Facebook, etc: it will get you banned. Don't try to do it on these mammoth organizations like LinkedIn, for example, which has approximately 700 million members in the US alone. It's a billion-dollar company. And they have anti-crawl code in their sites, and sentry bots that can detect when you're doing that and can get your IP address banned. So be careful with sites with programs like that.

Another effective way to market to people is going through Instagram, and clicking on someone's profile after searching by hashtag for #bookreader, #bookworm, or #booklover, for example. Go into their profile and click the Contact button, if it's there. The contact button will pull up an email address that is free for you to use and email, or you can simply contact them through the app itself by sending them a direct message.

Here's an email tip. Be careful and wary of spam laws in your country. The CAN-SPAM Act of 2003 is highly applicable to your marketing. If you're doing a mass mailing, you need to have an opt-out option programmed in there. When I do mass market emails through Zoho, for example, it automatically includes an *unsubscribe* or opt-out link: you've got to have those in any marketing emails that you use, or you're in violation of anti-spam laws.

Every time you get a warm lead, you have to harvest that email and you have to store it. Keep that email and follow up with that person. One of the mistakes I made from LinkedIn early on was that I wasn't following up with all these connections that I was making. I finally began establishing some relationships with readers that I followed up with later on. I think my initial connection with them was several months, or even a year, prior. I now make it a point to keep them on my radar.

You will never stay on their radar. They need to stay on *your* radar always.

This has worked over direct email as well. I will just go down my email list and re-establish communication with some former readers and express something like, "hope everything's well, hope you guys are doing well, especially now in the midst of this economy / pandemic / circumstance, whatever, etc. - hope you're staying safe." They reply, "I am! Thank you so much for asking - wonderful to hear from you! Hey, you know what? Son of a gun I actually forgot, I meant to buy your book!" Out of the blue. That would have never happened had I not reached out.

You have to remember to reach out. Program Outlook or calendar reminders to follow up with them. Follow up with readers you've connected personally with at regular intervals. And oh, my, all the *other* reminders you can program into Outlook! I have tons every week! Things like:

- Finish editing your new book – I highly recommend *Denouement Editing*[22], by the way: Janine is fantastic!
- Post daily creatives across social media
- Look through podcast groups on Facebook and see who wants to interview an author
- Record a chapter of your audiobook
- Produce a video for your quadrilogy
- Create a TikTok video sharing or reading some of your book
- Check sales metrics for books

All of these reminders pop up every day while I'm conducting my authoring business, helping me to stay on top of what I need to get done.

Be thinking about your visibility. Paul Strikwerda says "Being outstanding doesn't make you stand out. If people don't know you exist, don't expect them to hire you. If you really want to play the trumpet professionally, you better learn how to toot your own horn."[23] This is where you learn to market both continuously *and* shamelessly. And "hire you" here can be synonymous with "buy your book."

You have to be able to come to a point where you are okay with tooting your own horn and promoting yourself and your books regularly and shamelessly, because you're not promoting a product. Your product is *you*. You're promoting *you* to people. And there's a great amount of rejection possible when you put yourself out on the chopping block that way.

I want to be memorable. I want people to say "oh sure, I know who he is." Johnny Depp once said "one day the people that didn't believe in you will tell everyone how they met you". I love that phrase, because there are tons of people that you cross paths with in life. You want them to say something good about you. You'll want to be memorable. People often joke that they'll be able to say "We knew him when."

Readers are everywhere. We talked about the thrill of the hunt before. I love how I can go about my day out there in public and wear something that advertises with pride what I do. I was in Safeway the other day, and someone saw my shirt and asked me about my books. People go to my website from the vinyl lettering on my car.

Now, you do have to walk a fine line between exposure and overexposure. And only you can determine how much you're putting yourself out there. You will see the amount – and the types – of responses that you receive for the posts that you create. So if your posts are entirely business-oriented, and there's not a shred of personal connection points in there for humans – if there are no connection points for people to wrap their heart around, you're probably going to be unfollowed, you're probably going to be muted, you're probably going to be disconnected from…and you have to be careful about that. You're walking a fine line, so you personalize your outreaches, and you personalize your emails to leads, family, friends, potential buyers, everyone.

Be *social* on social media! That's what it was created for! Dale Carnegie once said "a person's name is to that person the sweetest and most important sound in any language."[24] It is amazing the amount of likes on *personal* content - video specifically - as opposed to static business images or ads that I place. As I said before about content being king, VIDEO is king. Post your pictures as *reels*, not just as still images. The difference in audience interaction is huge. Check out this link as to why to post your images as reels on Instagram as opposed to just a still image: https://www.lemonlight.com/blog/video-for-instagram-how-to-choose-between-a-feed-video-a-story-a-reel-and-instagram-live/. And here is a link for how to create some really good ones that skyrocket your engagement.[25]

People do want to take the time to watch videos of what you've put out. People are humans, and they like connecting with humans. Especially humans in motion. People like things real and genuine. This is why I don't particularly like programs like Hootsuite, because it's not "in the moment". And it's not how I'm feeling right now. I don't use those programs that auto-post your content at specific times. It's not spontaneous that way. Imagine the impropriety of posting a business blurb, splash, ad, whatever, wherever, and it happens to send – *because you programmed it to do so* – right after a mass shooting. You have to be really careful and really real and genuine with how, and where, and what you post online. The Internet never forgets.

Do you get birthday reminders for contacts on LinkedIn? Wish people happy birthday! Wish them happy anniversary. Congratulate them on their new position - that is being social. That is being human! That is recognizing people.

How would you like to have a tractor beam? The truth is that you already do. If you're using hashtags out there on social media, you're using a tractor beam to draw people to you. Hashtags are magnets. They are tractor beams: they draw your audience to you by using the associated words that your target audience is using in order for them to find you. It is very wise and prudent to use hashtags. I've made a practice of doing that.

One of the ways that I maintain good visibility is I post my website in as many online places as I can where I can get a quality backlink. Some good examples are Alignable, LinkedIn, Twitter, Reddit, Quora, Doodeo, SoundCloud (read chapters of your book on there and share them!), Craigslist, etc. By the way ads on Craigslist for your books – more on that below – are still very cheap and do get a lot of exposure! eBay as well!

But the point of all of this is that I want Google to see these and say, "Hey, there's authoraaronryan.com again! Oh, there they are *again!* Oh and there they are yet *again!*" And so I go, in quality and reputation, up Google's indexing. That's the way that SEO works. Google likes those links. News flash: it's called "the web" for a reason. Google likes good content, good traffic, your site being fully optimized and being really about what it says it's about: being content- and textually- rich. That's how you maintain good visibility.

The only 'person' I really need to see me before anyone else does is Google. If Google sees me, everyone else will start to see me.

Here's a case in point: Google likes Craigslist. You may not remember, but Google used to have a tool called PageRank. It was a little progress-meter bar in Chrome's shortcuts bar. It would measure from 1 to 10. Of course, Google had a 10 out of 10 rating, because, well, it's Google. Craigslist, I believe had a nine out of 10 at its peak. So, if you post on Craigslist, Google is going to index that too. And therefore you're going to be indexed not just in Craigslist, but also in Google, *because Google likes Craigslist.* One of the reasons for this is because Craigslist is almost purely textual in nature.

Perhaps you've never tried advertising on Craigslist, but I'd highly recommend it. It's $5 for an entire month for posting. I've posted approximately 15 ads at a time per month in the major Craigslist city markets across the U.S., and I've done that on more than a few occasions. $5 per month is great pricing and great exposure!

Also, Instagram and Facebook ads are low cost per click, and you can optimize with hashtags. Something to consider doing!

Now, far be it from me to promote visibility solely *online*. Join a Meetup! Visit meetup.com. If you're near a major metropolitan city, join that major metropolitan city's Meetup for authoring, if they have one. If they don't have one, create one! Writers Meetups are fantastic. In 2020, during the pandemic, you couldn't exactly get together monthly at restaurants and rub shoulders with fellow authors who are doing the same thing, but you could meet virtually online, and have webinars as well. Those are almost just as good. You couldn't break bread with your colleagues like you could in a physical Meetup, but those meetups are wonderful visibility: you can connect with colleagues, learn together, and also get referrals that way.

They're also really good for mixers. You don't have to join a writing Meetup. You can join a business Meetup such as what I mentioned before like BNI, Bizbuilders, Chamber of Commerce, etc. Those groups are great to try out. You may not want to join with their annual membership premiums and their monthly fees for this and that, but you can at least meet people once or twice before they require that you become a member. Get your visibility and your reputation out there and have them potentially refer you to others. You even get a free breakfast sometimes!

I believe in potentials. I believe in possibilities - that will be my epitaph on my gravestone: He believed in possibilities. I have an unquenchable belief in the possible. All of these so far are about trying out possibilities.

Find what *your* belief is.

If you follow my @authoraaronryan Instagram channel, you'll note a lot of different images and infographics that are often pop-culture related, or something to do with my family or whatnot. They're mostly about my books, because it's a business channel. And sometimes they have a humorous twist. I want those to be memorable. Post memorable and engaging content, and people will remember and engage with you.

YouTube and Vimeo are great avenues to maintain visibility and connect with people! If someone has posted a review of your book, *comment* on that video! Thank them for choosing you. Applaud them for a job well done! That way, people watch the video, and they see your comment below and say "oh hey, here's the author" - and then they have a convenient link to contact you by.

Or if someone has provided an interview of you, you can create a playlist in your YouTube channel and host *all* of your interview videos there in one channel. Are you hijacking their comment thread in so doing? I don't think so. You're merely pointing out that you were the author, and that you were proud to be part of it. I wouldn't call that hijacking. Mean what you say, and do it in a complimentary spirit. Also – ask if you can share these videos that you've seen your readers post. That way you get more exposure as well. And then you could potentially use those on your website in your portfolio.

Quora is another great site where you can ask and answer questions about being an author, whether posed by readers or by fellow or aspiring authors. It is yet another quality backlink that you can create in those postings, linking back to your website and content. Anytime you post anything anywhere, include your website and contact info in a signature when you can. It's so critical to do that. Get yourself *all* over the web. It's a bit creepy, but Google sees it almost everywhere, even in an email signature. I don't know how they do it – I don't want to know – but it's creepy and effective.

Contribute to your fellow authors. There are countless ways for you to connect with colleagues, to share what you've learned, and to learn from them; to dream together; to cast goals together; to show that it really is possible. You will only be a successful marketer and you'll want to increase your visibility and authoring, if a career as an author puts a *fire* in your belly. If you don't have that fire, you won't want to market and you won't want to be that incredible success. I *live*, *breathe*, *eat*, *sleep*, and *drink* being an author. Ask my wife: they're my passion and my delight. I *love* what I do.

I'm really fortunate that I've been able to write and self-publish all of the books that I've gotten to do so far.

An inspiration writer that I highly recommend is my friend Thibaut Meurisse. His book *Upgrade Yourself*[26] was a game-changer for me. That book is absolutely fantastic. It is a Tony Robbins-esque personal motivation compendium. It really rocked my world. I was very grateful! All of his books have been highly encouraging and motivating.

I want to motivate you as a business owner to develop *hustle* right away. Remember my acronym from before. I am often applauded for the hustle that I have, not just by fellow authorss, but also by readers and potential buyers that I reach out to who have actually said, "I appreciate your hustle. I admire your hustle. Good hustle," etc. I'm going fast. I'm working hard. I'm hustling to bring in bread to put on the table for my kids. So get that hustle, adapt it, own it. Make it part of your life in your approach for business, and you'll be successful.

WHICH ONE ARE YOU?

I want to outline the difference between hobbyists and entrepreneurs before we close this chapter out.

Hobbyists make hobby money. Maybe a bit of coffee money here and there. Entrepreneurs create revenue. Hobbyists are thinking it might be nice to have a bit of loose change. That name is not a coincidence. Entrepreneurs on the other hand are focused on building something that lasts; constructing something that has foundations for the long term.

I'll quote an author & voice actor friend of mine again, Paul Strikwerda: you don't want to attract "readers that expect a gourmet meal at a fast-food price and at drive-through speed."[27] You deserve more.

Lose the hobbyist and earn what you're worth!

Hobbyists have a pastime. It's an occasional fling. Entrepreneurs create an ecosystem. The former jump in every once in a while, subject to their emotions and whims; the latter erect a foundation that weathers time, economy, and more. It's building your home out of straw vs. bricks. There are only a few wise little pigs. Don't let the big bad wolf come blow down your hobbyist house of straw. This is not a leisurely activity that you pop in and out of. My author career is from 9am to 5pm Monday through Friday, just like a normal job. *Workin' 9 to 5, what a way to make a livin'…* Except *this* livin' is an utterly fantastic livin.' My authoring are done in a studio within an office, just like a normal career. They are growing and I'm moving up, just like a normal vocation.

Hobbyists dance around success; entrepreneurs *are* the success.

Hobbyists are a dime a dozen. They're the sheep. Entrepreneurs are one in a thousand. They're the shepherds. They're the pace-makers, the trendsetters, the goal-hitters.

Hobbyists follow along and aren't convinced that they need to take notes. "Give me a break, I'll remember this for sure." Meanwhile, entrepreneurs are scribbling detailed notes to refer back to.

Entrepreneurs take everything they've learned and assimilate it into a focused, tailored approach that is unique to their gifting and styles, enabling them to do what they know, and live how they can best grow in skill. They don't stagnate; they start producing, and people take notice. In the end, even chimpanzees have leaders that all the others follow.

Hobbyists have fly-by-night morality that depends entirely on what it will cost them. They don't see the need to obtain a business license because that means that they'll have to pay taxes on their hobby money. They see no need to get an LLC that will cover them in the event of a legal disagreement because of the one-time cost of $150 to register an LLC, which seems insurmountable to them.

Entrepreneurs, on the other hand, happily register their business with local, state, and federal authorities because they want to be established, and they firmly believe that paying taxes is the right and ethical thing to do. Hobbyists hope no one notices and seek to stay under the radar. Entrepreneurs take great pride in knowing how much they've made and knowing that paying taxes is what is required of responsible citizens.

Hobbyists think that what they do is good enough; entrepreneurs, on the other hand, are never satisfied. It's never enough! They go the extra step. Hobbyists use excuses like "It was good enough." Entrepreneurs would never say that. There is *always* room for improvement. There is *always* refining to be done.

Hobbyists see no need for a logo, branding, or any symbol of who they are. Their identity isn't wrapped up in their craft yet; so, there is no need to adopt a symbol of their greatness or their skill. It's futile to pursue any kind of epitome of their offerings; they haven't arrived yet at a place where they see their vocation of monumental importance yet.

Entrepreneurs, on the other hand, see a logo and branding as utterly definitive of who they are, and what sets them apart. They are *self-aware*, and know that providing great service doesn't make them unique; providing great service that is absolutely a cut above the rest is what they strive toward, and *that* is what makes them unique. Concordantly it's easy for them to look at symbols and choose something that demonstrates the qualities that they already, or want to, showcase. Lao-Tzu said, "When you are content to be simply yourself and don't compare or compete, everybody will respect you." Be utterly yourself. Be utterly even *more* than yourself.

Hobbyists look sadly at every cost, and wish that life didn't exact so much from them. Sometimes they're even looking for a handout. Entrepreneurs, on the other hand, look at expenses as *investments*. The problem hobbyists have with expenses is that they lack patience: they don't grasp that it first requires a willingness to plant a seed before you can watch it grow and enjoy its fruit. *They want the fruit, not the growth.* And sometimes, like Queen sang, "they want it *all*, and they want it *now*."

Any good thing worth pursuing takes investment. Entrepreneurs who have skin in the game know that their investment can pay back dividends. The pride an entrepreneur feels when they own something outright and bought it with their hard-earned dollars far outweighs the joy the hobbyist feels when they've been given a handout.

The entrepreneur feels gratification. The hobbyist feels relief. That relief, once put into words, would sound like "Phew! Dodged a bullet there. Almost had to spend some money!"

The entrepreneur can successfully say "*I* did this. No one else. *Me.*"

The hobbyist uses everything free and hopes that their readers and buyers will like the substandard product they churn out with all their free goods. Cheap and free stuff don't impress. Then they get mad and jealous of all those around them who are succeeding. They wonder why it's not fair, and they shake their fist at the world.

I know of one such aspiring author who I gave a *free* consult to that got everything for free and was expecting to succeed. The next post I saw from him? *He was asking his Facebook friends to buy Christmas gifts to his son because he couldn't afford it.*

Skin in the game.

Hobbyists have simple email agreements and handshake deals. Entrepreneurs seal their deals in blood, with contracts that contain clauses that protect their interests.

Hobbyists go for the one-and-done approach with their "readers." They're grateful for that one payoff and then goodness knows if they'll ever see that reader again. Entrepreneurs develop long-lasting *relationships* intent on future work. Their readers become "read" – past tense – and never read their work again. Entrepreneurs want to hang onto those relationships with those readers. Hobbyists hope their readers come back. Entrepreneurs *intend* for their readers to come back.

Hobbyists don't feel the necessity to create structure or anything that guarantees them a real shot at success. It's not a system for them; it's a random happenstance occurrence of maybes and hopes and what-ifs.

Entrepreneurs don't work that way: they don't *wait* for their dreams to come true; they *make* their dreams come true through concrete and comprehensive goal tracking and intention.

Remember, intention trounces hope every single time.

Hobbyists have fragile and limited payment avenues. They'll take PayPal and *maybe* Venmo. Even better, they'll just take straight under-the-table cash. Why report that to the IRS? Entrepreneurs provide their readers ease of payment, with multiple possibilities.

Hobbyists will unwisely, repeatedly write on their phones, because they don't want to invest in a good computer. Entrepreneurs will purchase what they need.

Here's the most important one. Hobbyists undervalue themselves. They'll allow themselves to be taken advantage of because they don't know the immeasurable value of their own service. These are the ones who will give away their books for free always, because they don't value the hard work they put into it enough to charge market value for them.

Entrepreneurs charge what they're worth. They have a firmly ingrained sense of deserving market rates, and charging rates commensurate not with their length of experience, but rather commensurate with what the service simply costs. It's not based on how long they've been in business, if the economy is on a downturn, do they need something on their resume, or feeling they somehow don't deserve it.

Entrepreneurs know the worth of their product, and they charge accordingly.

Hobbyists will charge well under market value out of desperation and wanting badly just to say readers "bought X number of books," when really, more to the point it would be "buyers *received* X number of books for free" on their resumé.

A entrepreneur knows that the book costs what the book costs…period, end of story. They're in it for passion *and* to turn a profit. It has to make sense, monetarily.

Now, all of that was not to knock hobbyists! If your goal is to just maintain a hobby and you don't want to do any of that for profit, so be it. Hobby away. I mean it!

INVISIBLE GOALS ARE NO GOALS AT ALL

If you wander aimlessly through your day, if you're kind of hoping and praying that this day turns out well and that you're a moderate success on some level, that's not a goal. Have concrete SMART goals like we talked about earlier.

Proverbs 29:18 says "Where there is no vision the people perish." Make sure you have vision going forward. Be on sentry, keep your eyes peeled, turn over rocks as often as – and wherever – you can, because readers are out there.

There's a verse in Proverbs that says "go to the ant you sluggard", reprimanding the sluggard for being lazy and encouraging them to look at the ant: it's harvesting. It's preparing all its food, it's storing up for winter. Smart little animal! Be that smart little animal: ask for reviews from readers, form a Yelp page, a Facebook page and a Google Local page. Not just your Amazon or Goodreads pages. Google sees these other ones and sees active reviews being posted on an active account with a website linking back to you.

One of my daily goals is to spend 10 minutes thinking of what else I can do to benefit both the authoring community and my own business. I don't do that every day. But that is one of my goals. What can I do to offer substantive content, to offer encouragement to help my colleagues grow? Again, I've been given a lot.

Once more, I have to come back to this. Try to look at purchases as *investments*, not expenses. This is a huge difference in perspective, as a business owner who wants to dream their business into reality. Every single penny you spend as an author is an *investment* into your success. It is not an expense. And the sooner you get away from that perspective, the sooner you'll see a membership to a writers guild…a promotion for your book….a graphic designer for a better cover…as no big deal. The sooner you'll see vinyl lettering on your car (the purchase of it) no big deal. The sooner you'll see a hat with branding on it as no big deal. Yes, they take a little bit of funding from you. But they allow you to *make* a lot of funding.

Most importantly, dream. This is not rigor. This is an incredible career that allows you to have fun, to create, and to be chosen. There's something wonderful about being chosen. When your book is chosen and someone purchsaes it, what an honor! It's *huge!* Dream this business true by treating it like a business.

Always dream of how you can improve. Always envision upgrading yourself.

Proverbs 29:18 says "Where there is no vision, the people perish." Make sure you have vision going forward. Be on sentry, keep your eyes peeled, turn over rocks as often as – and wherever – you can, because readers are out there. They *are* out there, and the money is out there as well.

Vision sees things into focus. And remember:

Your focus determines your reality.

CHAPTER 5: SUCCESSFULLY PROMOTING YOUR SELF-PUBLISHED BOOK

BEAT THE STREETS...AND THE CYBERSTREETS AS WELL!

In no particular order, here are a LOT of things that I do that have yielded success, and I pray they do the same for you.

SPECIFIC WAYS TO PROMOTE YOUR SELF-PUBLISHED BOOK

Amazon Ads

These come with the territory. If you're self-publishing through KDP, Amazon ads go hand in hand. They generated 57.2 million in sales in 2022.[28] Amazon has courses and support to enable you to develop decent ads, but where I've found better support is through Dave Chesson's Kindlepreneur. He's even reachable via email. He has amassed a huge following, and KDP itself even cites some of his work and recommends some of his courses in attempting to help authors publish their works and list them correctly. And the ads that you can run through KDP can be very fruitful – if you do them right. There is a method to the madness, so I'd highly recommend visiting something like Dave Chesson's course on Kindle ads at https://courses.kindlepreneur.com/courses/take/AMS/lessons/. The trick is of course making good content that people will be interested in.

One rule of thumb, promote your KINDLE book – people want to spend as little as possible. If they see that your book has value, and they've landed on the Kindle version, but they really like paperback or hardcover, once your blurb sells them, they'll switch and buy the version they want

TikTok Ads

TikTok is huge – and it will continue to grow, that is, until the US Government disallows access to them, if that happens. They have a huge reach. Sometimes you'll find that your posts on Instagram, LinkedIn, Twitter, Facebook, etc., fall on deaf ears, but if you use the right hashtags (i.e., variations of #fyp and #fypage etc.) in your post text, it reaches more viewers.

And as long as your ad doesn't contain any material that might be deemed controversial in some countries, you can quickly reach thousands and thousands, in fact hundreds of thousands, of eyes. It is an investment that has a big return and lots of eyes on your books. The trick is of course, again, making good content that people will be interested in.

Facebook Ads

I have not personally found Facebook ads that useful because I think for the most part people are conditioned to seeing ads in their feeds and scrolling right by. Facebook is the social media king, but our feeds have become proliferated with advertisements, causing us to skip them and move on down quickly to the personal content again from our friends and family. So use this one with care. Check out this article from Kindlepreneur on it: https://kindlepreneur.com/facebook-ads-for-books/

Organic social media content

All the time, do this. Do this, all the time. Seriously. Keep engaging your viewers. You may think or feel that you're really driving yourself into a hole, burning out, or falling on deaf ears, but ultimately, you're reaching people, and that's the goal. Post engaging content! Ask for comments in the video. Ask people to engage with you! Ask them to check out your website. Always list your website.

Social Media Aggregators

What are they? They help you take all of what you're posting online and put it in one place, so you can take your influence and increase your revenue. Check out this article to explain more:

https://getflowbox.com/blog/social-media-aggregator/

Social Hubs

Get a social hub like Dot Cards or LinkTree so all of your social media is in one place, and all of your channels fall on one page. Oftentimes the new WordPress sites that you create will allow you to post all of your links in a footer menu (at the bottom), and that's helpful as well. But for other social media links – or if you have a vast amount of them – it's a good idea to put them all in one place.

YouTube, Vimeo & TikTok

Make videos and post regularly! SO critical. Google owns YouTube. You post on YouTube and use your keywords and text to drive traffic to your website, and people. Put your keywords into your titles and descriptions. Put your website into your descriptions! So critical. And use the hashtags that will drive traffic to you. Some hashtags I frequently use are #yabooks #kindle #fyp #fypage #bookstoread #booksbooksbooks #bookworm #booklover #bookstagram #booktok etc.

Facebook & LinkedIn Author Groups

Be careful of this one. You don't want to market your books to fellow authors too much. They are not your audience. These people MAY buy your books, but it's not as likely because, again, they're not your market, and they're trying to market their own books as well. You're looking for READERS, not authors. But there are author groups that pair you with readers as well. And there are also reader groups out there, specifically, that are looking for new and creative writers to join their ranks and share their works. One group I recommend is "Connecting Authors to Readers ONLY" – it's at https://www.facebook.com/groups/authorsandreadersonly. This group is devoted to purging out all the scammers and con artists out there that only want to sell you marketing schemes and run away with your money. Unfortunately, many groups online are replete with them, so keep your guard up. Anyone that flatters you and invites you to DM them, be afraid…be very afraid. Make like that popular 90's beloved Hollywood character and… run, Forrest, run!

Reddit & Quora

These two sites, particularly Quora, are great to be able to answer questions on for new and aspiring authors who are seeking advice on how to start, or want Beta readers, or are looking for help on some aspect of running their writing business. By posting and answering their questions, you're increasing exposure and brand awareness, and making your mark as someone who is helpful and friendly in the industry. Reddit is great for community building just as in the Facebook and LinkedIn author groups I've mentioned.

A great one on Reddit is at: https://www.reddit.com/r/selfpublishing/ or at https://www.reddit.com/r/selfpublish/ And of course there's the KDP community at https://www.kdpcommunity.com/

Craft fairs / Trade shows / Vendor markets

I cannot stress these enough. DO THESE. You will make pennies on the dollar for any book you self-publish that sells in KDP, Ingram Spark, Barnes & Noble, Kobo, Smashwords, etc.. That's just how it is. You will make FAR more if you sell direct to people. So encourage people to go to your website where they can find out about the story and purchase a signed copy from you directly. It is SO much fun sitting there and greeting people as they come by, and having someone stop by and allow you to share what your story is about. In so doing, they will also find the links (provided you've put them there) for Kindle, audiobook, etc., and if *that's* their preferred venue, so be it: they'll go there instead. But at least this way you funneled them to your site. They may just sign up on your blog while they're there. And speaking of...

Blog

Already stressed how important this is. SO critical to build a following. You can do that and amass a large number of supporters.

One word of caution: you should work now on developing some thick skin because it's always the people you never thought would unsubscribe who do: namely, family and friends. They are the last people to support you, and that's just a sad truth. They'd rather monetarily support the rich celebrity who doesn't know they even exist than someone who is local to them who they know. Not that you need to make videos where you're begging for their support, mind you, but just develop some thick skin in this regard. At any rate, blogging should come natural to you – you're a writer!

So, write compelling content about your life, about your writing journey, about what's happening along your road right now, and take your readers with you there. Invite those whom you meet at craft fairs to sign up on your blog as well! Put a clipboard out for them to sign up on – it DOES work!

Occasional free giveaways

Nothing wrong with the occasional free giveaway! I'm generally not excited about giving anything away for free, but do things like offer a free book for a review online. Offer a free book to the first three people who sign up on your blog.

Promotion services

Services that run promotional campaigns to their thousands and thousands of readers, such as Written Word Media, Bookbub, Book Raid, Book Barbarian, Fussy Librarian, Pretty Hot Books, Self-publishing reviews, etc.: these are GREAT. They do drive traffic to your site through sending out emailers to their readers, and you reap the rewards of book exposure and people actually buying your books. For a pretty hefty list of those who provide these promotions, visit this site: https://davidgaughran.com/best-promo-sites-books/

Editorial Reviews

Seek editorial reviews for your books. Those speak volumes from those in the industry who can write compelling reviews. I really appreciate The Bookish Elf, and highly recommend them. Their reviews are SO good. They're detailed, you can tell they read your book, they're comprehensive and enjoyable to read, and very flattering. They also have a large following! Others include:

- Self-Publishing Reviews
- Book Nerdection
- Book Review Directory
- Kirkus Reviews
- Many Books

And so many more. Some of them are very expensive, and you won't be accepted by all of them, but just know that an editorial review can speak volumes about your novel from a trusted source. Onlinebookclub.org is another one but I have had mixed results from them, and I've even had a few authors include spoilers in their reviews, which is awful and that reviewer clearly didn't have much experience.

Book signing parties with Family and Friends

With the caveat of what I said above, family and friends should be included in book signing parties. Use Punchbowl or Evite invitations to invite them to it, and they'll come! They'll celebrate with you. Especially if you're buying the pizza.

Vinyl Lettering

Why not? You're driving down the road, you get rear-ended because someone was trying to read your vinyl lettering and they went right to your website while screaming down the highway at 85. What could go wrong? Seriously though, we all know they were screaming down the highway at 85 in order to keep up with YOU, who were screaming down the highway at 85 just to get home and start hammering out that new novel you just had an awesome idea for.

Vinyl lettering is free advertising on a moving billboard. One of my favorite things is to get stuck in traffic, where everyone around me can see "The War Is Coming. Visit getthesebooks.com." How cool is that?!? They go to my website and realize that it's an awesome sci-fi quadrilogy (or tetralogy if you prefer) and they can find out more about it. Why not? It also helps make your car's mileage a deductible business expense.

Custom T-Shirts

One of my favorite shirts to wear says "You are dangerously close to being killed off in my novel." Another one says, "Writers Block: when your imaginary friends won't talk to you." And yet another says, "I Make Stuff Up." And still one more says, "Anything you say can and will be used in my novel." I love wearing these. I feel pride in my career while wearing them. They elicit conversation from those around me. They're a conversation starter…about my books! Why not? Why do I want to wear Nike and Adidas all day, and advertise for *them*, when I can advertise for *ME?*

Business Cards

Business cards are not dead. You'll need these for mixers and meetups. And for trade shows! I'm always surprised how many people take my business cards at trade shows. But they're showing interest, and they want to check back in on my books at a later time. Business cards are a small footprint for a big impression. Design these well. Use your picture, your logo, your contact information, your pictures of your books, your website, etc. – all of it! Take the time to make them shine. Make them different from other people's cards! This is your calling card to tell people what you do and allowing them to take you with them.

Bookmarks

Bookmarks are a highly common giveaway that a lot of authors make. So make yours unique! You're marketing to readers! Readers have books. Books need bookmarks. Your bookmarks should have your website, a picture of you, a picture of your books, etc., and are a great way to drive traffic back to your site.

Flyers

I love handing out 8.5x11 flyers at trade shows, or mailing them to bookstores, or putting them on car windshields. They're great advertising because they also drive traffic to my website and show people what I do, what the book(s) is about, and they're designed in such a way as to foster interest.

Vinyl banners

You'll definitely need these if you're going to host a trader show or vendor market booth. This could be a wonderful backdrop behind the table you're sitting at. It's also great for library book signings, which leads me to my next point…

Library Book Signings

Most local libraries will let you hold a book signing. Granted, if you're not in Libby or in their official system, they can't 'endorse' you or your book, because you're not actually in their library. But they will let you have a free conference room to hold a book signing in, and that's great exposure for local patrons. You're just usually not allowed to sell your own books onsite; they have policies against that. But they, like your local Barnes & Noble, are all too willing to help out local indie authors. Same with local smaller bookstores.

Neighborhood Facebook groups or Foursquare

Foursquare connects you to local residents as do Facebook community groups. For example we have a private Facebook group specifically devoted to the small community in which we live. We can post things on there to reach those fellow residents, and share what's going on in our lives. Foursquare will connect you with locals as well.

Author Pages

Make sure to make an author page on Amazon, Goodreads, Medium, AllAuthor, and Bookbub, etc. All of these are optimized, all of these allow you to describe who you are, list your books, etc., and increase your social presence online. With Goodreads, they aggregate information on your books from KDP, so you'll want to monitor those and make sure they have the correct book covers, descriptions, and titles that KDP has. With Amazon's author page, specifically, it will show you a count of your followers, which is also great. And speaking of Medium…

Posting articles and excerpts on Medium and LinkedIn

You can use these sites to post articles and excerpts of your books, which is remarkably helpful for increasing exposure PRIOR to them going to your book page, especially if it's keyword rich in the title, subtitle, and descriptions, and allow links to your author or book pages.

A+ content on Amazon

If you self-publish through KDP, you have the option to create A+ artwork for all of your books, and all of your series, to allow you to further differentiate your books from others,' and to make your book stand out with imagery. A+ Artwork must be approved by Amazon, but what you post offers a nice way to give your book page some 'pop' as it were, and allow it to stand out with compelling artwork.

Only Paperback or Hardcover?

The answer is no. If you choose to only produce in paperback or hardcover (KDP does not allow this; you'll need to produce it as an eBook as well) you'll be leaving a LOT of money on the table. The overwhelming lion's share of my sales stem from Kindle eBook versions. Those are the most appealing because of the mainstream preferred way of reading nowadays, which is digitally. As CD's have given way to streaming, books have given way to eBooks. Kindle is a great way to promote your book, and you don't have to set the pricing so low that it's maddening to you or feels like a sellout. The truth of the matter, however, is that there are tons of people out there who still love the feel of a good book in their hands (preferably hardcover), and if they buy and like the Kindle version, they very well just might invest in a hardcover, a blankie, a coffee mug, and a fire to sit by and enjoy it all together! But do start with Kindle.

Also, make sure you're timing the release of your audiobook – and use the Audible credits you get to pass on to interested parties who would like to try Audible.

Audiobooks

A large contingent of book readers are those who will only 'read' them in audiobook format, either in commutes to work, or while they're working. Audiobooks are another revenue stream you can create to funnel more sales to yourself. "Adapt and overcome" they say, and so you must. You'll lose out on Kindle, hardcover and audiobook sales if you only sell paperbacks. You'll lose out on audiobook, Kindle and paperback sales if you only do audiobooks. You'll lose out on audiobook sales if you only do print and digital. It's actually pretty affordable to hire a good competent voiceover artist (I know; I'm one of them!) through royalty shares. Meaning, if your book sells, then they get paid. Or they can do a per-finished-hour pricing to narrate your book. For me, I narrate my own, and I'd HIGHLY suggest you invest in good recording equipment and audio treatment of an existing space you have, and record all of your books. Nothing will connect your reader to you quite like your own voice narrating your own story. And why shouldn't it? They're your creations, your children, it's your world you built, and all of that. No one will love your material or be more enthusiastic about it – or narrate it quite as well – as you will. Audiobooks are another revenue stream you just can't afford to ignore.

Soundcloud

What? Isn't Soundcloud just for musicians? Nope. Especially if you narrated your own audiobook, or if you have the rights to post the narrations of other voice talents who have recorded your books, then you can post those to Soundcloud and attract listeners to your books that way as well. And it's yet another way to post your website and attract people to your story. Trust me, you want as many sources out there as you can get to drive traffic to your books.

Fiverr

Despite the fact that Fiverr has almost singlehandedly become the "F" word in the creative industries and driven down pricing for multiple industries, you can find some pretty dang good creators on there who are willing to provide you with interviews, blog articles, press releases, book cover creators, book blurb creators, Facebook ad creators, Amazon ad creators and optimizers, and so much more.

For the marketing side of it, you can meet some great creatives who are very talented themselves at writing, and they can help to create interviews for you with fantastic questions, allowing you to highlight your work in their interviews, and drive traffic to your book pages and your website.

Kindlepreneur

He's not God, but Dave Chesson is a great resource for some pretty holy self-publishing work. Kindlepreneur has LOADS of resources and Amazon-vetted blogs. He's has proven experience in providing great ways to increase your book's exposure. He puts out a fantastic product called Publisher Rocket[29]. Visit Dave's site at https://kindlepreneur.com/. I have learned a ton of good solid information from Kindlepreneur, and I like that he takes the time to write informative blogs *and* keep in touch with his readers if they write to him.

Facebook Click Testing

Steve Pieper has a pretty vetted course that does take time and money, but if you are an investor, and willing to be patient and try, you can explore his methods for Facebook ads click testing, and be able to really optimize your ads to see what works, and sell a lot more books than you would just through Amazon ads or TikTok ads alone. Check out Click Testing at https://clients.stevepieper.com/ammo-front-door-with-testimonials/ Please note! I have not personally tried these, but I have heard nothing but good reviews, and it's on my plate of things to do.

ARC readers and Beta readers

ARC (Advanced Review Copy) readers and Beta readers are absolutely crucial to your book's success. You will want to have people ready to post a review right after it's released and get yourself on a good footing of reviews that attest to the quality of the material therein. ARC Readers and Beta Readers serve this purpose well because they get the copies of the books before they are released to the public, and they're the first ones that can comment on it and leave a review for it.

Timing of your Releases

Make sure that you time the release of your book(s) with any promotions and press releases or blog articles or radio interviews that you do, so that they all line up. That just maximizes on the timing of your release and makes the whole thing fresh in the readers / listeners / viewers' eyes.

Title & Subtitle Keywords

This one is so critical. I saw my books shoot up the charts once I did this. Don't be afraid to use keywords in your title, in your subtitle, in your book description, and in your keywords themselves of course. Don't fear keyword stuffing for now! Amazon, is, like Google, a giant search engine! The approach is the same. Use those keywords to optimize your listing and have people find your content! For example, my book used to be called "Dissonance Volume I: Reality." That's it. Now it's called "Dissonance Volume I - Reality: Post Apocalyptic Dystopian Alien Invasion Book Series." Look at all those keywords in there! It's loaded! Those keywords in the title match the keywords in the book description, which match the keywords I've selected, which match the categories that I've posted the book in. You have to remember that Amazon is a search engine. If you're wanting a book to be findable, all of the details about it need to agree with each other.

Way back in the nascent days of the Internet, people would design a plumbing site and use keywords behind the page like "Britney Spears," thinking that people would be searching for that and would find their page. But this tactic doesn't work. Sure, people were searching for Britney Spears, but once they found a plumber's page, does that make them happy or upset? They're going to get confused, and bounce. Google got wise to this tactic.

Just like a website where you have to have the title tag, meta tags, alt tags, body text, and keyword density agree with each other or the site won't get found in the search engines, your book's details all need to agree with each other or the book won't be found in the Amazon search engine. Make sense?

Allauthor.com Book Cover Of The Month Contests

Allauthor.com has great book cover contests you can vote on. You can submit your own covers for the various categories that pop up, and people can vote on them and thus increase your exposure of your books. Pretty simple strategy, and it's always a nice confidence booster when people like your cover. After all, people still judge books by their covers, right? Allauthor.com cover of the month contest is at: https://allauthor.com/cover-of-the-month/

Series Promotion

Many authors make the mistake of running promotions on every single book in their series. Let me put it to you straight: there is NO point in promoting anything beyond book 1 in a series. If Book 1 was good enough to have sequels made from it, then let them be standalone. If it's good enough, then your reader will then go on to buy Book 2, 3, 4, or however many there are. You should only be running promotions and driving traffic to Book 1 of your series. Anything else, people will arrive there and wonder why this is a successive volume in a series and where the heck is the first one? And they won't go digging for it. In this microwave day and age we live in, people want to be taken right where they want to go, and lickety-split. Too many clicks, and they'll bounce. But, on *another* point about a series, make an omnibus edition! If you have a series of books, I highly advise putting them all into *one* version, and then selling that at a slightly lesser price. People have snatched up my *"Dissonance"* omnibus all-in-one Kindle box set sometimes quicker than the independent installments in the series!

Review Videos

The reviews that people leave for your books? You can make videos of those, simply by grabbing their text, copying and pasting it into your video editor, and making review videos that you can upload to your YouTube account for viewing. People will see those and then be able to see a *lively* review of your book. That's a nice visual representation of what someone said. You can see examples of how I've done this at https://www.youtube.com/playlist?list=PLMnbc3h716btKQ1LWC4PajP9HQkew-B1t. These do help because people are visual. You can set the video to a cool catchy soundtrack, and it increases the visuality of it.

IG Book Influencers & Book Reviewers

Instagram (and other places) have tons of book reviewers and book influencers with very large platforms. They might be an enthusiast for lots of different things, but if books are one of those things, then by all means contact them and set aside a budget to have them promote your book. Make sure that their following is large, that they appear to be genuine, real people, and most importantly, that their posts are being engaged with / liked / favorited / whatever. Bots don't favorite influencer posts. 😊

Guest Appearances on Podcasts

Podcastguests.com! Matchmaker.fm! Podmatch.com! Great places to form an account and profile at, and then you can message (or be messaged by) podcasters! With podcastguests.com, every single day I receive possible candidates to appear on for a podcast interview. I've had some of my best ones come through these funnels! Lots of podcasters out there are seeking to interview special guests, and some of them, specifically authors. Some of them have nothing to do with writing or authoring; they just want anyone with a very cool life or career story. And you better believe that I apply for those as well, because inevitably I'm (or they're) going to steer the conversation toward my books and authoring, which makes me very happy. You can also find podcasters and interviewers on Fiverr who will interview you, but for a fee of course.

Multiple Self-Publishing Sources

If you self-publish through Kindle Direct Publishing and you choose the exclusivity option of Kindle Unlimited, you will be locked into a 90-0day do not compete clause. One of the advantages of choosing KU is that you can have expanded distribution of your book, and you're paid a small percentage on KENP (Kindle Edition normalized pages) as far as pages read. But you can do expanded distribution just as easily, by publishing simultaneously through KDP AND Ingram Spark AND Draft2Digital. One of the ways you accomplish this is by purchasing your own ISBN (International Standard Book Number) # for each edition of your book FIRST through bowker.com or myidentifiers.com. This site will allow you to purchase packages of ISBNs so that you can attribute one to paperback, one to hardcover, one to eBook, one to Audiobook, if you wish. And that way, you can put your books on multiple self-publishing sites Simultaneously. Through Ingram Spark, for example, you can get yours into the library systems AND in Barnes & Noble. Through Draft2Digital you can get them into Smashwords, Apple, Google Books, Kobo, and more. There are advantages to expanded distribution, but there are also disadvantages of course. The main one being that if you ever need to make a change in your book, you'll need to re-upload your new version of that book in multiple places all over again. So make sure that you have it edited well, that all mistakes are gone, and that it's as near as perfect as possible before you submit. These three sites will keep track of the sales you've made and send you periodic revenue reports from units sold.

Written Word Media has a fantastic article on so many ways to get yourself out there. Check it out at: https://www.writtenwordmedia.com/100-book-marketing-ideas-for-authors/. I've used them to great extent over the years for some really wonderful promotions. They do cost, but they do drive traffic to your books! They are a well-respected industry source for effectively bringing your book into readers circles.

That's it! But not really.

That's about it. but not really. There are *tons* of things you can do to market your book! TONS. Use your brain. Be creative, because that's what you are! Just remember: everything you spend is an *investment*, not an expense. Be willing to just t*ry try try try try* – try new book descriptions for a week! Try new book covers for a week! Try new keywords! Try using keywords in your titles and subtitles. Be willing to try new things and experiment! It's SO important to be adaptable and flexible in this industry! You don't know unless you try.

Like Dory said, "just keep swimming, just keep swimming."

CHAPTER 6: NETWORKING & MENTORING

GRAPES GROW BEST IN BUNCHES

We've talked about creating and sustaining a thriving writing business. We've talked about marketing and visibility as well.

Now it's time to continue that growth, to expand *outwards*, to connect with colleagues, and to talk about something that's so critical to refining your craft – and that's mentoring and community. I cannot even begin to stress how essential these are. But I'm sure going to try. The hubris of the newbie says, "How hard can this be?" Let me tell you now: it's hard. You need mentoring. You don't just pick up a keyboard and magic happens and all your wildest dreams come true. This is not Oz.

> *"Success isn't about how much money you make. It's about the difference you make in people's lives."*

Before we discuss mentoring, however, let's talk about another component that's critical for you. It's called *networking*. You may have heard the phrase before:

"grapes grow best in bunches." It's very true! There are lots of communities online today that you can join. And you, as a grape, can join your fellow grapes and grow well together. There's a sweetness to be found in clusters. There's a sweetness to be found in these thriving communities where you can actually connect with colleagues, see who is on the same career trajectory that you're on, bounce ideas off them, ask about equipment, training, conferences, mentoring, books, resources, tactics, approaches, whatever, and receive valuable feedback from those who have gone before you. You don't know it all yet. You probably never will. I don't either.

As I discussed in a previous chapter, it's important to duplicate, it's important to receive feedback: *honest* feedback from people who have gone before, who have been down the road that you are setting out upon, and to learn from them. There is nothing more valuable or formative than that for your writing business.

Grapes grow best in bunches. Be a grape, and be part of the bunches of the grapes around you.

There are a few quotes that I wanted to share with you as we kick off this chapter. The first one is by Zig Ziglar:

"You can have everything in life you want, if you will just help enough other people get what they want."

How's that for making sure to connect with others, to put their needs before your own, and to look out for your fellow man?

Michelle Obama also says:

"Success isn't about how much money you make. It's about the difference you make in people's lives."

Love that one. We talked about networking before, but you can have all the success that you want and still be a complete island unto yourself. You can be completely cellular - insulated in your own little world. If you stay that way, you end up as Gollum. Don't be Gollum.

It's so important that we get out of our own little bubble and rub shoulders with those who are trying just as hard as we are, who are succeeding just as well (or not as well) as we are and learn from them together. It doesn't do you any good to be a Lone Ranger. Even he needed his Tonto. There are Tonto's out there that want to give. There are people out there that need to receive - and you have been qualified to give and receive from birth.

I love the quote by MiSha. She says, *"Networking is not collecting contacts. Networking is about planting relations."*[30] How true is that? It's about planting seeds, watering them and ensuring that they grow.

I want to tell a little story about how I got started really going full bore into voiceovers several years ago. I reached out to an old friend of mine in high school. I knew that he was as an voice actor, but lost touch with him and his family. But I knew through the grapevine – *there's grapes again!* – that he was doing voiceovers. So, I went to Google, went to his website, contacted him and said, "Hey, I'm thinking about finally launching full-time into voiceovers. I was wondering if you could help me with any advice or tips." And he wrote back and said, essentially, "Good to hear from you...talk to Scott Burns."

Wait what?

That was it! It was like two sentences. Just that little bit of brevity. And then he was gone. It was the strangest and most blessed thing, in the long run. Right then and there, I remember thinking, "uh... okay, I don't *know* Scott Burns. I know *you*; may I talk to *you* please?" It was so interesting – and a little discouraging from the very start – to be farmed out right away. I had been outsourced, or *offloaded* perhaps is a better word. But boy did fortune strike in that moment, because I found out quickly who Scott Burns was.

I will never forget sending him an email that was very brief, and getting a reply back from him that was *mammoth*. And it wasn't a mail merge email; it wasn't "Hi NAME...nice to meet you NAME...it's good that you're interested as an author, NAME... allow me to help you, NAME..." No. It was all personalized. (That's the way we should be marketing, by the way. Ultimately, we can't afford to use any kind of "ready fire aim" approach when we reach out to people. We need to take the time, strategize, and personalize our messages.)

His email contained personal answers to my personal questions, and he just gave and gave and gave - the man is a fantastic mammal. He is a walking exclamation mark, and if I leave my wife for anybody, it will be for Scott Burns, my voiceover mentor.

Honey, if you're reading this, we're together forever, and Rick Astley and all of that stuff, so don't worry.

Scott Burns is a wonderful man. He's very generous, and I'm so fortunate to have him as my mentor. Giving to others is not everyone's bag, I get that. Not everyone has the same *generosity* streak. Scott is a tremendously generous individual, and he comes to epitomize for me what is really *beautiful* about true community: some people are so willing to give, and so willing to help. You are their competitor of sorts, and yet they're still willing to help you. That's a beautiful thing. It's a *wonderful* thing.

You're joining a community full of lots of people like that who give to others, review your writing, answer your questions, point you in the right direction, etc. They want to share your own experiences, share your successes and your failures.

It is so important to be absolutely honest as far as where you've been in the journey, and this helps someone else avoid pitfalls and roadblocks and canyons to fall into. We're not all lemmings here; we're pursuing a common goal. And we want to help each other not fly off of a cliff.

Here's where Meetup comes into play again. You can network with colleagues through a Meetup in your nearest metropolitan city, or connect with your colleagues online virtually. It's great because you can get together monthly at dinners, break bread with colleagues, talk to people sitting across from you, learn from their mistakes, share ideas, ask questions, find out what works for them, and apply it to your own life.

The meetups and mixers are all excellent community-based organizations that allow you to connect with colleagues and really ask those important questions to learn, grow and rub shoulders with greatness. In so doing, greatness can rub shoulders with you, *and rub off on you*. You learn from those who have gone before. These are people that I consider role models.

So, get out there! Commiserate with your colleagues, learn from them, teach them, grow together. Grapes grow best in bunches.

Another way you can connect is by joining writing contests or cover contests. You can sign up for those and do the "Brady Bunch" Zoom-style lineup of all of you in a grid, read specific scripts that you've brought, and receive feedback, praise, critiques, etc. You receive what you need to hear in order to perfect your writing craft. Clubhouse is great for this as well.

We live in an era right now where there are far too many resources available to us online for us to actually fail. The resources are infinite; they are immeasurable. You can look online and simply Google "writing group", and you'd be shocked to find the sheer plethora of resources that are available to us to learn and grow together. They are on Reddit, Quora, Facebook, LinkedIn, Meetup,

Clubhouse, direct websites, online communities and forums, and so much more. It's amazing.

> *"The key is not the will to win. Everybody has that. It is the will to prepare to win. That is important."*

Participate in those Facebook groups, those LinkedIn groups, those Reddit groups or any other groups that are of benefit to you. Get in there and give and receive, learn and impart, converse and participate. There are *so* many resources to help you grow.

I simply don't know how people way back in the dark ages of writing in the late 60s did it. Ha! The online (and offline, as a byproduct) support community that we have now is just magnanimous and phenomenal. So please don't be an island unto yourself. Get out there.

Ray Kroc, the founder of McDonald's said, *"When you're green, you're growing, when you're ripe, you rot."* And how true that statement is! It is imperative for us as authors to continue learning. You're never done learning until you're you're pushing up daisies. We're all on a constant journey together of learning trends, seeing delivery styles change, things going in and out of vogue, adapting to change, rolling with the punches etc, in terms of assimilating new trends.

This is an industry where you're in great need of rejuvenation, affirmation, and encouragement. In the midst of the depression and frustration that you can endure by virtue of constant marketing and constant auditioning, we face a lot of rejection in this industry. As an entrepreneur, you face rejection anyway. But we face a lot of it in this industry in particular, through all of the marketing and auditioning we're constantly putting out. Moreover, you need shots in the arm in order to get that replenishment of energy and affirmation to keep you going. It's very crucial in this industry to rub shoulders with people that can give you that shot in the arm.

A PERPETUAL EVOLUTION

Let's talk about mentoring. I am not a mentor, nor am I about to sell you a mentoring package. Have I considered it? Yes. But with everything else I do, I don't really have it in me and I don't really have the time. I'm much more a mentor and an encourager as well as an auditioner and marketer. I'm the guy on the sidelines, with the pom-poms going *rah rah, you can do this*. I've foregone the spandex, of course, so don't worry. But I want to be on the sidelines being an encouragement to you!

There are a lot of people that migrate to the authoring industry, because they were told they write well. I have had that said to me exactly zero hundred and zero times. I don't remember, to ever having been told that. One more time: I'm a businessman who *happens* to write. I just happen to be great at it, and I accept that. But so many people come into this industry assuming that it's easy.

I'm appalled when I talk to a newbie, and the subject of mentoring comes up, and they brush it off. Their hubris gets in the way and they say, "Oh, I don't need mentoring. I mean, how hard can this really be, right? I really don't need mentoring. I know how to write."

You may know how to form sentences, but to form a compelling story may just be beyond you.

Rookies do that to their utter peril. Mentoring is part of the fundamentals of authoring. It's your first – and potentially your *only* – investment as an author. Not everyone who gets into writing should be doing writing, and it's a mentor's job not to lick your fingers and tell you things that you want to hear. It's their job to tell you one of three things:

- you got it (meaning don't pay me anymore because there's nothing I can ethically charge you to teach you)
- you don't got it (meaning don't spend a dime as an author because it ain't gonna happen)
- you don't got it, but here's how you get it (meaning let's talk about a roadmap to success for you, which will require some investment of course)

It's a mentor's job to drop you if you are 'unmentorable' - not to keep taking your money. It's also their job to drop you if you're already there, if you're already ready to deliver your stories compellingly, and not keep taking your money.

I'd like to share a few quotes with you about mentoring, and the importance thereof. These come from well-known mentors and motivational speakers.

John Wooden says "a good mentor can change a game; a *great* mentor can change a life." (italics mine)

Timothy Galloway says "Mentoring is unlocking a person's potential to maximize their own performance. It is helping them to *learn* rather than teaching them." You've heard the phrase "you can give a man a fish and feed him for a day, or you can *teach* a man to fish and feed him for a lifetime."

Bobby Knight, mentor, says "the key is not the will to win. Everybody has that. It is the will to *prepare* to win. That is important."

I absolutely love this last phrase!!! It is the will to *prepare*. So many people gravitate to writing because it "looks fun." It looks neat. *How hard can it be?* And they just want to get in front of a computer and type out a crappy book or slap something into OpenAI or ChatGPT and hope that it will make them millions. They're using *zero* innovation, *zero* self, *zero* ingenuity, and *zero* creativity. The computer is doing it for them. And they want it all for free. How many of their competitors *have* invested time and money and resources into obtaining quality mentoring, equipment, software, and resources? Do they honestly think they stand a chance at being heard?

In my humble view, there are five important purposes a mentor has.

Mentoring is designed to help you:

- determine the true meaning of what goes into a good book, to get underneath the words, to really figure out what you're really supposed to say, and how you can express that well
- get under those words and make them jump off the page at the reader
- breathe life into your story, to make it come alive, so that they are no longer just words on a page
- for audiobook narration of your stories, to *so* believe what you're reading that your *readers* believe you too

Now, there are definite differences between a good mentor and a bad mentor. A good mentor will be able to bring out the best in you; they'll be able to determine where your 'money' voice is, and where your signature sound is.

Also, a good mentor can help you figure out where that voice is going to be the most marketable, to help you find the most successful genre to enter into. You might think you have a great writing ability for nonfiction work. And your mentor may say "No, no! Your style is perfectly suited for romance! Or a memoir!"

A good mentor will be able to keep in touch with you and monitor your progress. A good mentor will want to follow up with you on occasion; a good mentor will *remember* you and be *proud* of you.

And finally, most importantly, a good mentor will *not* take credit for your success. A good mentor is there to help *you* be great, and to actually *exceed* them. A good mentor is there to pass on what they've learned, and enable you to be incredibly successful. They will not take credit for your success; they will truly enjoy watching you soar.

Now let's talk about a bad mentor for a second. Unfortunately, in many industries – the authoring industry notwithstanding – there exists many a "mentor" that is not meant to be a mentor; such people are, in fact, predators.

They'll make many promises. They sometimes have expensive mentoring bundles or packages. It's someone who usually knows just enough to make them *dangerous*. They think they have all the answers by spending a little bit of time in the writing industry in soaking up what they've learned. And so they pass it on, and they want to charge for it. But they're not the people who will sit with you beyond the confines of your pre arranged time, i.e., you have a mentoring session from 3pm to 4pm, and they're firm about finishing it right on the dot. Once I was in mentoring with Scott Burns, my voiceover mentor. It was 4:15pm. We were scheduled to finish at 4pm. He asked me excitedly "you're doing great! Wanna keep going?" And out of respect for him I said, "Oh, no, no, it's fine. I appreciate it! We've had our hour!" Scott didn't care what time it was. Conversely, a bad mentor will want to cut you off as soon as they can, and get back to what they were doing. They don't have a vested or genuine interest in seeing you succeed. Scott was okay with continuing past the allotted time frame.

I recently had a "run-in" with someone who has been doing writing for less than a year and is already 'mentoring.' They are putting out horrible amounts of misinformation and endorsing all kinds of incorrect and substandard tactics and relationships… they are leading people astray. It's maddening to see this. The only consolation is that they are receiving *plenty* of blowback from seasoned professionals calling them on the carpet.

And let me tell you about even one more bad example. There was another individual I knew who wanted to get into mentoring. I heard from three individuals who sent works to her, requesting that this 'mentor' review them. She had offered to review them! I'm told those people never received replies from that 'mentor'. "Yes, send me what you've written; I'll be glad to review and give you feedback!" Crickets.

These people never once heard back from her, presumably because they hadn't paid a cent to her. Such a 'mentor' didn't have their best interests at heart, and doesn't ultimately care. Additionally, her background did not include writing! Yet she felt she could mentor authoring, even though they she was just entering the field.

There's a phrase that I heard from my mentor once, and it's pretty funny! It is as follows: "It's been said that those who can't *do* writing *teach* writing, and those who can't teach…teach *shop*."

I'm going to mention again what Dr. Ian Malcolm in Jurassic Park said: "your people were so preoccupied with whether or not they *could* that they didn't stop to think if they *should*." That phrase comes to epitomize bad mentors. Bad mentors are so preoccupied with whether or not they could, that they don't stop to think if they should. Someone who has what it takes to be a good mentor will honestly *question* whether or not they would make a good mentor. Why? They obviously are too humble to jump into that role – they want to make sure they're ready first. A good mentor will know if they should be mentoring. And on the learner's side, as the Bible says, "A tree is known by its fruit."

One of the ways that you can really determine if any mentor is the mentor for you is to *vet* them. This is why Facebook groups, LinkedIn groups, Reddit groups, etc, are so important for you as a budding writing talent. They're also good for one who wants to go back to the drawing board and perhaps relearn the essentials from a mentor within the author community.

There's a long list of greats. This little list doesn't even come close to incorporating everyone.

Trust is a huge thing in the writing community as far as learning from those people who've gone before. If you can't trust them and what they're offering you, then you can't really expect to take their ball and run with it nor be successful. Again, you're *duplicating* a mentor. If you're duplicating a crappy mentor, you're going to produce crappy results, and you're going to receive (and put out) crappy information. And sometimes there are mentors out there that are labeled serial purveyors of bad information, because they perpetually misinform. Other times you'll run into someone on social media who just thinks they know absolutely everything. They're crabby and belittling in their replies. They're patronizing and insulting in how they deal with you. These people are unteachable. *Stay teachable.*

No one knows everything, simply because everything always changes.

You have to be really careful in who you choose as a mentor, and learn the correct methods for approaching writing. Your very first expense as an author could potentially be your very *last* expense. Mentoring could potentially save you thousands and thousands of dollars. They save you money by being honest with you if, in fact, you simply don't – and *won't* – "have it." Some people think they have it, and they are convinced that they should be a writer, when they just simply shouldn't at all…and they beat their head against the wall vainly and futilely. A sound mentor can spare them that agony.

A mentor's job isn't just to direct you to the best writing software. It's to help you really understand the industry so that your books will sell.

Here's an example. I don't like cats. My wife has a cat. We have a running joke that "we live at our home…with our dog…and her cat." But I don't really like cats. If I am writing a book about a cat owner who loves cats, then that character better freaking sound like they freaking love cats….because I don't!

I'm a fiction writer. It's my *duty* to make my readers believe my characters. If my readers don't believe my characters, they won't believe me. Did you get that? It's my job to read about kitty litter so *compellingly* that these people who read my books are going to say, "Wow, that Aaron Ryan guy knows what he's talking about! I want *more* books by Aaron Ryan!" That is my job: to write so compellingly, even if I don't really care about the subject matter. That's my job: to bring those words to life, and make it believable.

Your first expense as an author is getting mentoring in order to help you find your own signature style, be believable, write compelling material, and understand the industry. Don't spend all this great inordinate amount of money on equipment, resources, memberships, conferences, workshops, etc. It should be *mentoring* from the start. And then if your *mentor* determines that you are viable, that you're marketable, that you have skill and talent that is ready to go, *then* you start hitting the pavement.

Ultimately, you want to constantly learn. You're never done learning! Remember what Ray Kroc said. There are plenty of things that you can learn; plenty of new practices, new techniques, and new approaches you can adopt in order to stay fresh.

I'm still learning things. You find little nuggets of truth all the time, everywhere.

Don't just cruise through your day and churn out half-assed writing. Stop and learn and soak up and sponge what people – your colleagues and your mentors and teachers – are putting out there, and how they're doing it. The same goes for how they conduct marketing. Keep on learning. Your career depends on it.

It's so important to network and continue to grow and refine yourself as authors. It is an art. It is the greatest career you will ever have. And I mean that with all my heart.

CHAPTER 7: TO AI OR NOT TO AI: THAT IS THE QUESTION

CONTROVERSY! FIRE AND BRIMSTONE! TAR & FEATHER HIM!

Disclaimer: I already know this is going to be a long and most certainly controversial chapter for those who have been involved in the authoring industry. Breathe easy.

ARTIFICIAL VS. REAL

A.I.. It's the wave of the future, right? Everyone seems to be fearful of it, and yet everyone seems to be embracing it in one way or another.

> *We can govern our emotions and figure out what approach is best for ourselves, not condemning someone else for an approach that works best for them.*

Ultimately, I've used A.I. graphic designers to design characters for my novels, to bring them to life and visualize them so I could use them in promotional materials, and so on and so forth. That doesn't endorse it, but it also doesn't make me sleeping with the enemy.

A.I., as with most tools, *can* be used for good. The issue is when it is used to replace good, hardworking humans.

Let me take you down a different path for a moment, if I may. I've mentioned that I'm a voiceover artist. In 2024 alone, at the turn of the year, almost as if someone had flipped a switch, I saw my voiceover career flipped almost entirely on its head. I *knew* already that several factors were impacting my bottom line as a voiceover artist. In 2023, we had the following issues:

- The SAG-Aftra strike
- The Economy
- Lowballing clients
- Underbidding colleagues
- Ad budgets spent
- And of course, A.I.

But when 2024 hit, again, a switch flipped. Suddenly the jobs were drying up and I was generating about 30%, on average, of what I would usually generate in a week. Granted, some weeks more than made up for it, because that's the way it is in many cases for entrepreneurs and sole proprietors: sometimes it can be feast or famine. It definitely wasn't famine yet, but it was certainly no longer feast.

What do I think is mostly responsible?

A.I., hands down, and I'm not kidding in the slightest. It's singlehandedly done the most damage to my voiceover career.

If it A.I.n't human, then it A.I.n't for me

Long live humans. Long live creative souls.

We live in an age of A.I.. Every day, more and more services spring up promising revolutionary and innovative results using artificial intelligence. The authoring industry is not immune to this. I've had works plagiarized before, and someone can easily take a general concept, throw it into ChatGPT and have it spit out a form-factor cookie-cutter recipe book in minutes, package it, and throw it up onto Amazon to make a quick buck. Is that creativity?

Not one iota.

I've actually churned out a lot of books in 2024. As such, I've been accused of having used A.I. to do so. Nothing could be further from the truth. When you're driven, and you type 102 wpm, and you're desperate to shift gears from a potentially failing line of work and would like to perhaps keep your home and not have to move, you pivot, and find a different career. So, I returned to writing, and published everything I had previously written and which was available in my troves. The *Dissonance* sci-fi quadrilogy, however, is all brand new and entirely original as well. Not one bit was written with A.I. I am inordinately proud of what God gave me in the *Dissonance* series. It is a powerful, epic story, and I believe in it wholeheartedly.

The same is true with all of my books, really. I want every one of my readers to know that not once did I employ, nor will I *ever* employ, the use of A.I. to sculpt any part of any of my stories. Those who know me know that I am staunchly and adamantly opposed to such cheats, because A.I. is largely responsible for the erosion of my voiceover career, and the voiceover careers of many friends whom I hold dear.

Make no mistake: I'm very proud to be a verified human. You should be too. The ability to create is a gift that I was endowed by my Creator, and I will never forfeit that nor set it aside to propagate something synthetic and imitative.

Everything you've read by me in my "Dissonance" sci-fi trilogy, my sci-fi thriller "Forecast," any of my business books and ANY of my other works, is 100% entirely created by me, the genuine article. I'm a verified human, and always will be.

To my fellow authors, I urge you to preserve the sacred gift of human creation and never stoop to such lows. Always cherish this gift you've been given. If you encounter writer's block, take a break. Don't cop out. Don't take the road more traveled by. Don't cheat. Toe the line for all of us, and keep creation – *true* unadulterated creation – alive.

Now. Are we a community? Don't all of us have the very same goal of putting bread on our table for us and our loved ones? Sure, but at what cost? Will we compromise in order to do so? Or will we toe the line for the rest of the hardworking authors out there?

There. I've said enough. Are we still friends? Or will I be *persona non grata?* Time will tell.

Long live humanity.

Sincerely,

Aaron Ryan,
Verified Human

CHAPTER 8: THE PROCESS OF SELF-PUBLISHING

THE NITTY GRITTY

The actual process of self-publishing is fairly straightforward, or, at least it has become so for me. It won't be the same for everyone, but in a step-by-step process, this is how I do it, nearly every single time the same way, and the usual order I do it in, though some elements may skip forward or backward a step or two. Hope this helps!

PRIOR TO PUBLISHING:

1. When the overwhelming majority of your book is written, convert it to a PDF along with any associated artwork and submit it to the US Copyright Office at the following link (choose your username and password upon registration): https://eservice.eco.loc.gov/siebel/app/eservice/enu?SWECmd=Start – YES, you have a copyright of sorts with an ISBN number. But plagiarizers are out there, and should it ever come to a legal matter, I would want the US Copyright Office behind me to

ensure protection of that which I've worked so hard to write.
2. Purchase editorial reviews for your book – these take time for the writers to write a good and compelling review, and you'll want to use excerpts of these on your book cover or in the book itself
3. Line up Beta Readers and ARC Readers in prep for your launch
4. Contract a graphic designer to design the cover, unless you can do it yourself
5. Schedule a virtual book tour through agencies such as RABT at www.rabtbooktoursandpr.com
6. Finalize your book, which means editing, proofreading, ensuring all chapters begin on odd numbered pages so they all appear on the right, etc.. Use a professional editor. This can take a few weeks, so plan accordingly.
7. Ensure that each version has its correct ISBN # (and appropriate US Copyright #, if you have it yet) listed in the front. Also include a disclaimer if yours is a work of fiction, something along the lines of "This is a work of fiction. Any similarity to actual persons or events is purely a coincidence."
8. Make sure you have a website and ecommerce in place. Hire a designer if you don't know how to create a good working website. And for ecommerce, you can always refer them to a well-known ecommerce site like Square or Stripe, that allow you to create listings for products fairly easily. I use Square, because Square lets me create a "storefront" page where the items I created can be featured, and you setup options for fulfillment alongside that. Or, you can go a much simpler

route and just take payments via Venmo, Cash App, or PayPal, etc..
9. When that's done, setup a pre-order period and a launch date & event. The pre-order period is what you'll promote to generate excitement for your book and offer it at a discount. The launch date and event are exactly what they sound like. The launch date is self-explanatory. The launch event can be *multiple* events. I've held them at coffee shops, restaurants, libraries, conference halls, and peoples' homes. It's very easy that way! You can set up the event in a site like Punchbowl or Evite and send out invitations to friends, family, and business associates.
10. Share the snot out of your upcoming book on social media. BE SHAMELESS. Share and share away, and be an enthusiast when you do it! Share tantalizing sneak peeks at the log line, or the full cover, or a sound byte, or you reading from a chapter, or paste a chapter in your posts if space allows. Be creative! And make sure it's all in line with your author branding, logo, mission statement, and who you say you are.
11. Credit the graphic designer in the front. Credit the copyright holder. Credit the copyright and include a warning for unapproved copying or reproducing in any form.
12. Purchase promotions through services like Written Word Media to time with your book launch
13. Purchase written interviews, podcast interviews, press releases and other forms of exposure from vendors on sites such as Fiverr, to be released concurrent to your book's release

14. Use Publisher Rocket through Kindlepreneur to find the best keywords to use in my title, subtitle, description, and keyword fields themselves, applicable to my book's content. Also use Publisher Rocket to determine your proper categories for your book. Amazon *may* (probably *will*) change these at various points in your book's lifespan as it sees fit, but that's to ensure that it sells. Publisher Rocket allows you to search through Keywords, Competition Analyzer, Category Search, AMS Keyword Search, and has several tutorials to help you succeed. This is *really* helpful software that has enabled me to zero in on my preferred categories, analyze my competition, assess which keywords have the best chances of succeeding in the market, and loading my ads up with the right targeting. Highly recommended!
15. Purchase ISBNs for your book through https://www.myidentifiers.com/ - especially if you're not using Kindle Unlimited and don't want to just use the free one that KDP issues you. If you get your own, you can use the same book across multiple platforms: KDP, Ingram Spark, Draft2Digital, Kobo, etc..
16. Observe the proper formatting for Ingram Spark for their cover templates. They are different from KDP and require different production standards, and they can definitely be finicky with your finished artwork, rejecting it multiple times. So, make sure you use their cover templates
17. Work with a book description writer, someone who is vetted and has produced attention-grabbing and successful book descriptions prior to yours. Use

these book descriptions on Amazon, Ingram Spark, Draft2Digital, everywhere. Be wary of phrases like "Buy now before the price changes!" as you're not allowed to use such vernacular on IS and D2D.
18. Contract someone to generate ad-worthy artwork and copy for ads on Amazon, Facebook, TikTok, Instagram, wherever you prefer. Make sure you get someone who can properly format your ads and make them visually appealing and targeted. You'll also need to set a reasonable budget because you can burn through it quickly.
19. Create your A+ content and artwork that you can then upload to your books once they're published on Amazon. Here is a great article on that: https://www.junglescout.com/resources/articles/amazon-a-plus-content/
20. Begin recording the audiobook, if you so choose. This doesn't have to be available right away. Also note: you WILL find further errors in your book when you record your audiobook version. It's just par for the course. Be ready to republish a corrected version as you go through it and record it, making note of the errors and correcting them in your manuscript.

IT'S TIME TO PUBLISH!

1. Convert your book to its various formats:
- Paperback (PDF)
- Hardcover (PDF)

- Kindle – I use Kindle Create, but you can use other .epub designing software
- Audiobook (mp3 files) – if you need someone to perform quality assurance on your files to ensure they are compliant with Audible's standards, I highly recommend Luis Aponte at leaponte91@gmail.com
2. Perform a final proof on each PDF version to ensure that each version looks good before uploading.
3. Determine the cost that you want to sell each of your books at. Make sure the price is competitive with other books of similar genres, and in line with fair pricing of similar books. Do **not** overprice your books! Be very careful. Here's a great article from Ingram Spark on your book cost.[31] *You* may think your Kindle book is worth $99.99. I'm exaggerating of course, but the reader won't. Price them strategically and fairly.
4. Visit https://kdp.amazon.com/ and follow the steps to upload each version of your book. If you start with the Kindle version, that is *highly* recommended, because then you can copy everything you entered for the Kindle version to a paperback and hardcover version. KDP has cover templates they can give you, just as Ingram Spark does, based on the type, layout, and page count of your resulting book, which will help you make sure everything is aligned, including the spine.
5. For Ingram Spark, use their cover generator to generate your cover. Ensure that your document is compliant with their standards including for photos embedded in the document itself.
6. For Draft2Digital, decide your eBook pricing and where all you want to distribute it in electronic form.

7. One thing to keep in mind is that your pricing should be consistent for each format across all venue where you're hosting each version of your book. Customers don't want to buy your book on one site only to find that it's lower – or worse, *drastically* lower – on another site, after they've purchased it.
8. Claim your Amazon author page at: https://author.amazon.com/claim/join. Fill out your author profile, your about-the-author section, all of it, and have it ready.
9. Consider price promotions if you want to offer your book introductorily at a lower price, or for free, although as mentioned earlier, I don't recommend the latter.
10. TELL THE WHOLE WORLD ABOUT YOUR BOOK!

AFTER PUBLISHING

1. KEEP TELLING THE WHOLE WORLD ABOUT YOUR BOOK!
2. Ensure that all of your descriptions posted correctly, especially if you had sections of your descriptions that were bold, italicized, in a larger font, etc.
3. Ensure that your categories are correct, especially where KDP is concerned. Again, please note that KDP will arbitrarily change your categories from time to time, where they feel your book is more fitting and where they feel it might sell well. Just go with the flow and don't fight this. It's an uphill battle you don't need. As long as your title, subtitle,

description and keywords all match, people will find your book when they search for it.
4. Market the snot out of that puppy, using advice and direction provided earlier in this book.
5. Verify at intervals where and when your book published. Draft2Digital will send you individual notices where your eBook has been published, just FYI. You can take all these links and post them on your website as *additional* places where readers can find your book(s). You truly do want to provide as many opportunities and locations for readers to buy your books. Readers may only prefer to purchase through Smashwords. Or Kobo. Or Barnes & Noble. Or Kindle. Or Audible. Or Vivlio. Or Trulia. Or…wherever. The more places you make your book available, the better your distribution, and the better exposure you receive, thus, the better sales.
6. From time to time, be willing to experiment with different book descriptions and categories. If your book is not selling well, find out why. Dave Chesson with Kindlepreneur has a great article on this and ways to troubleshoot sales issues, at: https://kindlepreneur.com/book-sales-problem/
7. Make sure to get the KDP Champ app at www.kdpchamp.com: I highly recommend it! It's a great app for receiving notifications when your book sells, *which* book sells, and showing you your cost-to-profit margin if you're running ads on your books.
8. If your book begins to really sell, you'll want to contact a literary agent for representation. Agents are a business too; they want to make sure you're making money before they take on the burden of representing you, putting their name on the line, and

investing money to promote your book and your author persona. Don't expect a reply right away. They can take a while to reply. And if they don't reply, just move on. Most of them will ignore you unless they fell your material is inherently "saleable" meaning they think bookstores and publishers will be motivated to take it on. Before you approach them, make multiple mini versions of your book such as the first 3 chapters, the first 50 pages, the first 10 chapters, the first 20 pages, etc. All of them have different standards, tastes and preferences for what they want to read. You can use a site like QueryTracker[32] to form an account and approach the ones that want to work with your genre of literature. Here's a great article for how to approach them: https://writingforyourlife.com/how-to-approach-a-literary-agent-for-representation/. Give this time. It's not the end-all-be-all. It is *wonderful* when one responds favorably to you! But don't hang your hat on that. Make your own fire. Don't get frozen in time and wait with bated breath for any one agent. I have five agents as a voiceover artist, but those all took time to be included on their rosters. It didn't happen with my first pen stroke.

As with all things, there is *so* much more that I could say, and there is too little that I could say, and there is too much that I could say. There's a great article by PublishDrive that spells a lot of this out, and I highly recommend you check it out at: https://publishdrive.com/how-to-market-a-self-published-book.html

Ultimately, you are a creative. You are someone who creates. Therefore, I urge you to *create* ways to sell. Think outside the box. Be willing to stretch yourself and be flexible and color outside the lines. You don't have to sell in only the same places where everyone else sells. There are so many places to sell! Find them. Find your readers. They're out there.

The most important thing you can do as an author is be yourself. Again, Oscar Wilde said, "Be yourself; everyone else is already taken." So be you, by all means. Don't try to be Tolkien, Collins, Lewis, Rowling, Asimov, Foster, or any of them.

Let those author inspire you, sure…but follow you own path, and make your own mark. You have a unique and powerful story to tell, and no one can tell it quite like you can. Your life experiences, your perspectives, your opinions, your insight, your education and everything that makes you *you* makes the story *the story*. Tell your story well and know that there are people out there who will want to read it.

TWO WORDS OF CAUTION

1. Hybrid & Vanity Publishers

Everything always changes, and methods evolve. One method that has evolved negatively, in my humble opinion and in the opinion of *many* in the author-sphere, is vanity, or hybrid publishing. Know two inviolable truths from the get-go:

1) no legitimate publisher will contact you out of the blue to offer to publish your book
2) no legitimate publisher will charge you a cent to publish your book

Vanity publishers are publishers that charge you a fixed fee, spread over several months, to publish and "market" your book. But your book won't get published at all until they've been paid in full. (I have emails to this effect from vanity publishers.) However, the consensus in authoring groups is that the marketing is never what they promised, and they end up charging you even more fees in the end. They do *not* have a vested interest in seeing your book succeed, because they've already made a pretty penny – some to the point of several thousand dollars – to get you on their vanity publishing roster. *I do not recommend vanity or hybrid publishers at all.* They will take your money and they may get your book published, but for the reasons I've stated before, you will lose some creative control (even though hybrid publishers tell you that you won't), you won't be able to negotiate your prices, it will take a while, and the startup costs are very steep. And sometimes, they pay your royalties only twice a year! Do you want to wait that long? I certainly don't.

A vanity publisher doesn't like the name given them, so they'll often hide behind the name "hybrid" publisher. Make no mistake: they're one and the same. Avoid at all costs, that's my counsel, and it's largely the consensus of the authoring communities at large, because people at large have had poor experiences with them.

They "do" what you could just as well do yourself, but they charge you an arm and a leg to do it, and no one will **_EVER_** market your book(s) like you can. No one will **_EVER_** be as enthusiastic about your stories as you will. Sell them yourself. They expect *you* to market your book, and they explicitly state that, even though "marketing" is largely "included " in their packages.

These guys will offer you slick, snappy packages with polished PDFs and peppy flowery speak in order to lure you in, with "testimonials" from happy authors. They are the minority: a drop in a bucket, if they even exist. They make you feel special that you've been "chosen;" but nothing could be further from the truth. You're not "special" to them; you're meat.

For the bargain price of up to $10,000 for some, you can be taken to the cleaners. Again, make like that beloved Hollywood character, and "Run Forrest, Run!"

2. Scammy Marketers

Community groups and forums are *replete* with them. They have bizarre names like "Blessings Smith" and "Olupawe Makitumba" and other usually Nigerian names. They have glossy photos that look like they came from a professional photo shoot. The truth of the matter is that these photos are stolen, and reverse image searches show that they are wolves in sheep's clothing, masquerading as perfectly legitimate marketers, in order to lull you in to some marketing plan, which is nothing more than a money-grab. They laud you with praise and heap acclaim upon you with ridiculous Facebook posts such as "O WORTHY AUTHORS, POST YOUR BOOK COVERS HERE FOR PROMOTION!" in all-caps and large typeface over attractive backgrounds. Nearly everyone who comments on their posts they'll reply with some variation of "DM me." It's pathetic. It's so old and tired, their approach.

Make no mistake: these are not reputable *or* legitimate marketers. They promise you the world and will give you heartache. They'll build you up to tear you down, buttercup. And one of their most disgusting new ploys is to masquerade as perfectly legitimate authors! You'll feel special that Suzanne Collins, the author of *The Hunger Games* is personally contacting *little old you!* How awesome, what an honor! It's not Suzanne. His name is Jonathan Smith, and his picture is of a woman. ??? Or his name is David Erick. Or Daphne Michelle. Why they continue to go for the two-first-name monikers is beyond me. They're all pathetic and deplorable. Granted, it just might be the actual author who wants to engage with you, if they're not quite a celebrity yet. Use probing questions such as "What was your favorite book to write?" "Tell me about your favorite character from that book?" "What is your favorite chapter from your book, and why?"" "How old is your protagonist?" And other variations like that. Largely, they won't have drilled down to such detail and won't have a freaking clue about the books that the *real* author wrote, whom they are impersonating. If they invite you to DM them, you know it's most likely a scammer. Ignore 'em and keep writing.

Watch out. The wolves are out there, and they're howling for your attention to lure you in for a kill.

Stay alive out there.

CONCLUSION

THAT'S A WRAP!

Thank you so much for reading this. I pray you get vision and clarity for your authoring endeavors. Terri Apple said: "Having a great voice isn't enough. Learning what to do with it is the key to a long and lucrative career."[33] Amen to that! You have a great voice that has told a great story. So tell it. Use that voice of yours to tell it well and share it well.

I hope and pray this book has been greatly illuminating, inspiring, and empowering for you as a budding or established author, and I pray that it's been helpful for you to market your book as well as your writing business.

Don't get caught up in awards or getting your book converted to a screenplay just yet. Let things happen. Breathe. For me, I don't want or need acclaim, statues, or fame. What would I do with a little golden statue anyway? Admire it for a few weeks and then put it up on a shelf and *maybe* notice it here and there?

What I notice is people repeatedly buying my books. I notice a new reader following me. I notice connections. I just simply want to provide for my family doing something that I love. That's my aim, and I've accomplished it for several years now.

I don't do anything else now except authoring and voiceovers. I provide both full-time, and my goals are in place to continue to improve and grow, and I will stick to them. I have an innate sense of hustle and *drive* that cannot be extinguished easily, save by staying up late because of my two boys, and then desperately craving sleep the following day.

I am *pulled* back into my office to get work done. It's gravitational. It is my *pleasure*, my *joy*, and I *love* what I do. That pull drives me to succeed. I love to work hard and smart, and I love to give of my knowledge of how I do so. I hope you have received just a smidge of that through this book.

Remember again what author Thibaut Meurisse said: success is not an event. It's a *journey*. My plan is to stay on that road. May it never end. May the success journey *never ever ever* end. *Ever.*

I want to be a *tremendous* part of your success. That's why I wrote this book: to pay homage to those who have been a great part of my success, and to edify them, but also to encourage you that you *too* can continue the legacy of success and far exceed what I and so many others have been able to accomplish in this business called writing.

May all your dreams come true in this endeavor, and may God bless you.

If you are an author, you are made of some pretty *stern* stuff. You are *resilient*. You have *tenacity*. You face rejection and insurmountable odds every single day.

You are putting yourself and all your heart and thoughts and feelings and neck out there on the chopping block, hoping people will like your book, appreciate it and leave a positive review. And yet, even when that doesn't happen, you somehow rise again, and stand tall above the smoking rubble around you.

You are compelled to create, so you dust yourself off, and soar into the heavens yet again. You steel yourself for the book writing task you face, and give it your all, because one thing is true: You are a *warrior*. You are a *dynamo*. You, my good writing friend, are a *freaking superhero*. May you be awarded book sales faster than a speeding bullet. Thank you for being in this battle with me, saving the world…one book at a time.

I cannot freaking believe I get to do this every day, and I have the utmost confidence that you can do it too. I believe in you. It's no mistake that the word "can" is in this book 285 times (now 286). It's because you truly CAN do this. (287).

There is *so* much more that I could say, and there is *so* much more that you and I both can learn. The writing industry is changing and evolving all of the time.

Running a business demands that you stay flexible, be willing to adopt new tools, and try out new avenues of marketing and outreach. It's all a giant maze, and a rolling stone gathers no moss. So…keep rolling.

Additionally, my way is not the only way. There are many, many paths to success, as long as you remember to treat your writing and self-publishing respectfully as a *business*. I hope that what I offered you in this book opens your eyes to the fact that you *are* more than able to do this as a successful business for yourself.

I am nothing special, just a little fish in a big pond, who decided to swim one way with all his might. If I can do it, so can you.

I also want to encourage you to be shameless. Don't ever apologize for sharing your story, or feel like you are trampling on anyone's free time or their patience. Share from the heart. Don't market to them. Be an *enthusiast* in your conversations with them.

Enthusiasts sell books. Marketers push them and promote them, but enthusiasts sell them.

And remember my mantra: your focus determines your reality. So? Focus. All the time, focus on it. Make it your focus, and that focus will determine your reality.

#youcandothis

WRITE ON! ☺

Please feel free to subscribe at my blog at:
www.authoraaronryan.com/blog for more information.
Feel free to write me at me@authoraaronryan.com.

You can also visit and follow my Amazon Author profile and follow me there at
https://www.amazon.com/stores/Aaron-Ryan/author/B0CRC2775Q

Thank you so much! ONWARD!

Love,
Aaron Ryan

ABOUT THE AUTHOR

**AARON RYAN: ENTHUSIAST
AUTHOR · VOICE ACTOR**

Aaron Ryan lives in Washington with his wife and two sons, along with Macy the dog, Winston the cat, and Merry & Pippin, the finches.

He is the author of the bestselling "Dissonance" sci-fi alien invasion quadrilogy, the sci-fi thriller "Forecast", the business reference books "How to Successfully Self-Publish & Promote Your Self-Published Book" and "The Superhero Anomaly", several business books on voiceovers penned under his former stage name (Joshua Alexander), as well as a previous fictional novel, "The Omega Room."

When he was in second grade, he was tasked with writing a creative assignment: a fictional book. And thus, "The Electric Boy" was born: a simple novella full of intrigue, fantasy, and 7-year-old wits that electrified Aaron's desire to write. From that point forward, Aaron evolved into a creative soul that desired to create.

He enjoys the arts, media, music, performing, poetry, and being a daddy. In his lifetime he has been an author, author, wedding videographer, stage performer, musician, producer, rock/pop artist, executive assistant, service manager, paperboy, CSR, poet, tech support, worship leader, and more. The diversity of his life experiences gives him a unique approach to business, life, ministry, faith, and entertainment.

Aaron's favorite author by far is J.R.R. Tolkien, but he also enjoys Suzanne Collins, James S.A. Corey, Marie Lu, Madeleine L'Engle, C.S. Lewis, and Stephen King.

Aaron has always had a passion for storytelling. Visit his website at www.authoraaronryan.com or the Dissonance quadrilogy website at www.dissonancetheseries.com

If you liked Aaron's book or the "Dissonance" saga, please visit the Amazon and Goodreads pages for this book and leave a positive review. Once it shows up, please email the screenshot of it to me@authoraaronryan.com for a discount on your next book purchase from him! Thank you so much! Reviews help SO much!

MORE BOOKS BY AARON RYAN

Dissonance Volume I: Reality

Dissonance Volume II: Reckoning

Dissonance Volume III: Renegade

Dissonance Volume Zero: Revelation

The Complete Dissonance Box Set

Reflections: A Compilation of Journals & Poetry

Forecast (WIP at the time of this writing)

The Superhero Anomaly

Running A Successful Voiceover Business

Five T's to Triumph in Voiceover Casting

How Do I Get Started In Voiceovers?

Voiceovers: A Super Business · A Super Life

Voiceovers: A Super Fun Pursuit

Voiceovers: A Super Responsibility

RECOMMENDED READING

I highly recommend the following books and resources for your authoring pursuit, business, or career:

Making Money in your PJs: Freelancing for Voice Actors and other Solopreneurs by Paul Strikwerda

The E-Myth by Michael Gerber

The Mastery Series by Thibaut Meurisse

How To Grow Your Small Business by Donald Miller

Self-Publishing for Dummies by Jason R. Rich

BIBLIOGRAPHY

[1] https://en.wikipedia.org/wiki/Kobayashi_Maru
[2] *Making Money in your PJs: Freelancing for voice-overs and other solopreneurs*, Paul Strikwerda, 2014 edition, page 369-370
[3] https://wp.nyu.edu/dispatch/2020/03/20/voice-over-trends-in-2020-and-why-voice-over-mentoring-remains-more-important-than-ever/
[4] https://www.quora.com/search?q=how%20do%20i%20self%20publish
[5] www.nethervoice.com/shop
[6] https://www.amazon.com/How-Self-Publish-Childrens-Book-Everything/dp/0997025492/
[7] https://www.amazon.com/How-Publish-Book-Amazon-2018-ebook/dp/B01M0J5KZA/
[8] https://www.amazon.com/Successful-Self-Publishing-Self-Publish-Market-Writers/dp/B07VC9J5JM
[9] https://thewritelife.com/writers-conferences/
[10] https://www.indeed.com/career-advice/career-development/how-to-become-a-author
[11] www.backstage.com/magazine/article/essentials-every-vo-audition-9190/
[12] http://users.cs.york.ac.uk/susan/joke/essay.htm
[13] www.foresthillretirement.org/stress-reducing-hobbies/
[14] https://www.imdb.com/name/nm3582255/
[15] https://www.kdpchamp.com/
[16] www.uptimerobot.com
[17] https://vellum.pub/
[18] https://www.autocrit.com/
[19] https://www.grammarly.com/
[20] https://www.amazon.com/stores/Joshua-Alexander/author/B086JNK8NK
[21] http://fractalfoundation.org/resources/what-is-chaos-theory/
[22] https://denouementediting.com/

[23] *Making Money in your PJ's: Freelancing for voice-overs and other solopreneurs*, Paul Strikwerda, 2014 edition, page 23
[24] www.dalecarnegie.com/en/courses/3741
[25] https://foundr.com/articles/social-media/make-instagram-reels
[26] www.amazon.com/Upgrade-Yourself-Strategies-Transform-Mindset-ebook/dp/B079VN6HK9
[27] *Making Money in your PJs: Freelancing for voice-overs and other solopreneurs*, Paul Strikwerda, 2014 edition, page 325
[28] https://passivesecrets.com/amazon-book-sales-statistics/#:~:text=Books%20are%20the%20most%20popular,genres%20on%20Amazon%20in%202022
[29] https://publisherrocket.com/
[30] www.linkedin.com/pulse/networking-collecting-contacts-planting-relations-misha-griffiths/
[31] https://www.ingramspark.com/blog/pricing-your-book
[32] https://querytracker.net/
[33] *Making Money in Voice-Overs,* Terri Apple, Lone Eagle Publishing Company (1999)

Made in the USA
Coppell, TX
11 July 2024